STRETCH THE CORNFIELD

STRETCH THE CORNFIELD

ROB KISER

State ✦ House
Press
Buffalo Gap, Texas

Library of Congress Cataloging-in-Publication Data

Kiser, Rob
Stretch the Cornfield
Rob Kiser
   p. cm.
ISBN- 978-1-933337-59-3 (pbk. alk. paper)
ISBN- 933337-49-1(pbk. alk. paper)
1. Football-Offense 2. Football-Coaching 3. Football-Texas-History. 4. Hal
Mumme 5. Football Coaching-United States 6. Football -Air Raid Offense
7. Football-20th Century
This paper meets the requirements of ANSI/NISO, Z39.48-1992 (permanence
of paper) Binding materials have been chosen for durability ♻ ∞
I. Title.
   "Cataloging-in-Publication Data available from the Library of Congress"

State House Press
P.O. Box 818
Buffalo Gap, Texas 79508
325-572-3974 · 325-572-3991 (fax)
www.tfhcc.com

Printed in the United States of America
Distributed by Texas A&M University Press Consortium
800-826-8911
www.tamupress.com

ISBN-13: 978-1-933337-59-3
ISBN-10: 1-933337-59-1

Book Design by Rosenbohm Graphic Design

CONTENTS

Photographs of the Iowa Wesleyan football team and individual players and coaches can be found on pages 66 to 71.

FOREWORD

"If a man has good corn, or wood, or boards, or pigs to sell, or can make better chairs or knives, crucibles, or church organs, than anybody else, you will find a broad, hard-beaten road to his house. . . ."

—Ralph Waldo Emerson

Through the years, this quote was eventually paraphrased to "build a better mousetrap and the world will beat a path to your door." From 1989 to 1991, Mike Leach and I used to say this to one another in the course of packaging and perfecting what is now known as the Air Raid offense. We set out to play football in a manner that would be fun to watch and play. This offense, to my way of thinking, had to rely on the passing game. Having started this project at Copperas Cove High School in central Texas, I was looking for a place to take the passing plan to the college level. Providence led me to Iowa Wesleyan College (IWC) in southeast Iowa.

A small (only 550 students) National Association of Intercollegiate Athletics (NAIA) school that had gone nearly two calendar years without a victory was the perfect spot to try all my radical ideas about offensive football. Dire circumstance is often the best scenario for innovation and on that level, IWC really excelled. Coach Steve Kazor, then an assistant for the Chicago Bears, called me and asked if I wanted the IWC job. Seems he was friends with the college president and could recommend me. After a month or so of talking back and forth, the job was offered to me on January 1, 1989, while I watched college bowl games at my home.

What follows is my account—along with numerous others—of how the Air Raid came to exist. I started out to create an offense based on the pass but what really got created was more of an *attitude* and not so much a collection of X's and O's. The players and coaches deserve the credit for this creation because they are the ones who executed the plan. Also, the people of Mount Pleasant, Iowa, and the surrounding area deserve kudos for fostering the environment that allowed us to succeed.

Coaches never invent anything—that ceased with Pop Warner and Amos Alonzo Stagg—coaches constantly reinvent the wheel. At that time, I was influenced by three great coaches. The first was Bill Walsh, from whom I learned to practice and game-plan. Walsh was a great teacher who found time to return phone calls and answer letters from the coach at an obscure NAIA coach in Iowa. The second was Mouse Davis, who started the modern run and shoot and convinced me that relying on the pass was the way to play offense. Davis's ideas about game adjustments were something I draw on to this day. The third and most influential was LaVell Edwards at Brigham Young University (BYU) who graciously allowed me to come study their offense year after year and provided me with the base ideas "I could hang my hat on." All three had a positive influence on my thinking and planning; all three were generous with their time and knowledge; and all three believed in the passing game as an offense.

During the three years I spent at IWC, Mike Leach and I would go anywhere just to learn teaching points that could help us build our mousetrap. Among the contributors were Dennis Erickson, Lindy Infante, Don Matthews, Bill McDermott, Roger French, Rob Ryan, Dan Lounsbury, John Jenkins, and Ronnie Vinclarek. Small points about the game often produce great results, and we were not going to miss any that could help us. The passion to produce a great offensive scheme was a daily quest at IWC.

The one fact that stands out about the Air Raid is that, at its core, it's an attitude more than anything else. It's an arrogant, in-your-face style that players love to play and fans love to watch. One of the most gratifying things looking back is the number of our former players who have gone into coaching and run the Air Raid. It's addictive, and we are all hooked.

It's also worth mentioning that members of IWC's roster who brought this offense into being went on to make contributions beyond the football field as doctors, lawyers, educators, developers, homebuilders, counselors, business leaders, and psychologists. IWC turned out all these professional people and more between 1989 and 1991. The catalyst for this success was a radical idea about how college football should be played. It started in a small stadium bordered by cornfields in Mount Pleasant, Iowa. An inherently hometown, mid-America mentality exists there that does not always react well to change. Fortunately, change was badly needed in IWC Tiger football, and the local population, which gleefully thought Hayden Fry an innovator for having the Iowa Hawkeye tight ends play from a two-point stance a few years prior, quickly saw the notion of having the whole offensive line play from a standing position as an idea they could embrace. Those Iowans were way ahead of the curve! So we named this book about thinking out of the box and stretching ideas to the max—*Stretch the Cornfield*—because that's what took place. First we stretched the ideas in a cornfield before the cult took hold nationwide.

Along the way, a group of successful adults emerged from a cornfield and are currently stretching professions from Minnesota to Texas and Polynesia to Florida, making the game of football and the way we played it the quintessential learning tool in their college lives.

We also diversified the small, sleepy campus, which had only one person of color when we arrived in 1989, into a multicultural place capable of putting on a luau complete with a roasted pig in the ground and lava lava attire or hosting a Texas chili cook-off. The usual Midwestern fare featuring Maid-Rite sandwiches was not forgotten in the process.

In effect, a campus with no diversity in 1989, would by 1991, have a harmonious team of players drawing on each other's backgrounds that included Midwesterners, Southerners, Tejanos, West Coasters, and Polynesians. From big cities and small communities, the 1991 IWC Tigers seemed to realize their destiny before it happened, and strength through diversity was the mantra.

To be sure, I was also blessed with great assistants at IWC, and most are covered in this book; but no one did more to make our offense and our team successful than the late Charlie Moot. He was a great coach, recruiter, and friend. He is still missed today. As you read this book, Charlie will come into focus as a great person who kept everyone laughing with his daily comedic exploits, intentional or otherwise. Charlie helped all us "crazy people to keep from going insane" as Jimmy Buffett once wrote. This book is dedicated to that late, great veteran of the Vietnam War and our defensive coordinator, Charlie Moot.

Enjoy!

Hal Mumme
August 2013

PREFACE

I met Hal Mumme when I was on spring break during my sophomore year at Elon University. A few friends and I were accompanying his youngest daughter, Leslie, on a trip to Hammond where Hal was the head coach at Southeastern Louisiana University. Both of us were big into history, so we spent most nights of that trip sitting at his kitchen table with a bottle of Maker's Mark talking football, politics, and Civil War history into the wee hours of the morning.

Three years later I was working at a hotel in Breckenridge, Colorado, when I got an e-mail from Leslie informing me that I should give her father a call. By then he was head coach at New Mexico State and looking for a new video coordinator to add to the staff. I took the job despite Hal's warning that I would "make about enough money to starve" and the fact that I had no video experience to speak of. The opportunity to work that closely with college football was an opportunity that I simply couldn't pass up.

My first couple months on the job were an unmitigated disaster, but some high comedy emerged from the rubble of my fledgling career in football video in the form of "The Gallup Chronicles," a journal I began keeping of the preseason and my professional foibles during the team's fall camp in Gallup, New Mexico. Public readings of my thoughts on the day in Aggie football and my latest audiovisual failures became a nightly staple in the hotel room where the coaches congregated after the day's double sessions.

A few months later Hal asked me if I'd be interested in helping him tell the story of his time at Iowa Wesleyan. He wasn't sure what form that story would take, but he figured it ought to be recorded by someone with a sense of humor. I jumped at the opportunity. From then on I got to tag along for dinners and nightcaps whenever former players and coaches from Iowa Wesleyan rolled through Las Cruces, furiously scribbling notes the entire time. I left New Mexico State the following spring before I made any significant progress on the Iowa Wesleyan project, but I hung onto the notes that I compiled in Las Cruces just in case.

Thankfully, the project was resurrected two years later when Hal started talking with Don Frazier at State House Press about doing a book on the story of the Air Raid. The following July I accompanied Hal to the twentieth reunion for Iowa Wesleyan's 1991 team Mount Pleasant, and ever since then a good portion of my life has been consumed by chasing down and ultimately telling the story that began to materialize that weekend. I never would have been able to grasp the full scope of this story without Hal's time and insight. We spent hours on the phone together rehashing events that happened during the original Bush administration, and if his memory ever failed (which was rare), he could always tell me exactly which former Iowa Wesleyan coach, player, or otherwise that would be able to help me connect the dots. More than anything, I'm grateful that he trusted me to tell story of the offense.

I'm also grateful for the efforts of everyone at State House Press who helped to bring this project to fruition. Thank you to Don Frazier for having faith in this project form the start, Scott Clowdus for keeping me moving in a productive direction, and Claudia Gravier Frigo who turned this manuscript into a book.

Special thanks to Mike Leach for being willing to go on the record despite being understandably weary of the notebook I've been toting around for the past five years. Mike Fanoga was also a huge help in mapping the landscape at Iowa Wesleyan as well as exceptionally understanding when I failed to deliver practice film to him in a timely fashion at New Mexico State. I remain grateful for his compassion.

Dustin Dewald was incredibly generous with his time and memories throughout this process. Other former Iowa Wesleyan players such as Marcus Washington, Chris Oepping, Marc Hill, Tim Smith, Jaime Luera, Bob Draper, Richard Morrow, Dana Holgorsen, Chann Chavis, York Kurinsky, John Coneset, Bill Bedenbaugh, and a number of others that I'm probably forgetting really helped to piece this story together by sharing their experiences, photographs, or anything else I may have asked of them along the way.

My efforts to check their accounts were supplemented by the stories of beat writers covering Iowa Wesleyan football way back when. I spent months poring through the online archives of the *Burlington Hawk Eye*, a local newspaper that covered the football program at Iowa Wesleyan during Hal's time there, especially Kalen Henderson. This story wouldn't look nearly as good if she hadn't told it so well the first time around. Her help in shepherding me around Mount Pleasant two summers ago as well as digging through her photo archives for the cover shots went a long way to bring this story to life. I am in her debt.

Bob Lamm was always available to field my phone calls and share his memories. I hope I'm as cool as him when I grow up.

Assorted stories on Smartfootball.com brought me up to speed on the significance of the Air Raid and provided me with the knowledge I needed to actually follow a lot of the conversations I overheard in the course of writing this project. Books that helped me to put me the story that came out of Iowa Wesleyan in its proper context include *Blood, Sweat & Chalk* by Tim Layden, *Swing Your Sword* by Mike Leach and Bruce Feldman, and *Play the Next Play* by June Mumme.

Many thanks to Matt and June Mumme for sharing their stories about what it was like on the home front while all of this madness transpired. I'd also be remiss to leave out Leslie Mumme, whose friendship put this book and plenty of other great memories into motion.

Most of all, my wife, Kaitlin, endured lots of nights alone over the past two years because I was holed up in a library or my office working on something that I rarely talked about. Somehow she managed to maintain her enthusiasm for this project despite my absence and the mystery surrounding it. I hope she's happy that I'll have plenty more time for dinner, drinks, cups of coffee, and sticks of gum. I know that I am.

Rob Kiser
Morristown, New Jersey

INTRODUCTION

I have to do what is best for the students. I have to teach them that it is important to go to class and get that degree. And I have to teach them something about life. These guys are going to be the kinds of friends to one another that you have for the rest of your life. And they are going to learn things here that will help them later on. We aren't just teaching X's and O's—it goes beyond that.

—Hal Mumme, August 1990

July 15, 2011 • 10:30 P.M. • Mount Pleasant, Iowa

"You guys gotta understand, you are the legends of Mount Pleasant," exclaims an exuberant Chris Oepping as he sets up shop at a table in the corner of a tiny sports bar packed with his former teammates, many of whom he hasn't seen in nearly two decades. Oepping was a freshman wide receiver at Iowa Wesleyan College in autumn of 1991 when the football team rattled off a ten-win season and earned what remains the tiny school's only berth in the NAIA playoffs. Since then, Oepping has called Mount Pleasant home, playing three more seasons at Iowa Wesleyan before joining the coaching staff for seven more. After that, he has worked at a local car dealership on the edge of town where he regularly recounts stories from the Tigers' 1991 playoff run to captivated locals who want to relive "the good old days."

On this night, Oepping's former teammates returned to the modest farming community in southeast Iowa from all over the country to be honored for their accomplishments on the football field from that fall of 1991. All of them have come a long way since that time. They're successful men with families, careers, and there's no longer a single flat top or mullet in the bunch. For most of the

1

evening's attendees, their last football game is twenty years in the rearview mirror, so they huddle around tables sharing updates on where life has taken them, recapping past exploits, and feeling the warmth of something they haven't felt often since their dream of a national title was snatched away on an arctic Saturday afternoon in Moorhead, Minnesota. As the evening wears on, Oepping takes a moment to look around at his teammates, sighs and flashes a thoughtful grin, "there was nothing that mirrored that moment, when the ball was in the air."

Unintentionally, he explained why twenty of his teammates left their lives hundreds and thousands of miles away to share a weekend together in a tiny town in the middle of cornfields. They came to remember a time when they had a goal that was so easily defined and so widely shared. In the moment that the oval-shaped ball was in the air, no outcome was predetermined and possibility abounded. Success could just as easily be snatched from an opponent as it could slip through their own fingers.

Scenes just like this one play out at watering holes all over the country on a nightly basis. Old men get together to escape the routine of their everyday lives and remember what it was like to be young men—their fates bound to one another and the possibilities presented by a ball spiraling above a football field. At most of these reunions, the recollections of past events and their consequences don't ripple beyond the table at which they're being told. The memories evoked by Iowa Wesleyan's 1991 team haven't just shaped the lives of the men sitting at this table; the events that inspired those memories have played a part in shaping the way that football has been played in the United States ever since their collective gaze was focused on a football hanging above Mount Pleasant's Mapleleaf Field.

When Hal Mumme was hired in January 1989 to revive a faltering football program at Iowa Wesleyan, the ball was most certainly in the air. The program had found some success in the early 1980s under head coach Tom Horne but went into a tailspin following his departure after the 1984 season. The Tigers bottomed out in 1988, going 0–10 during a season in which they managed to score only 76 points while giving up 316 points.

The administration at Iowa Wesleyan College hand-picked Mumme to turn around their school's fortunes on the gridiron. Mumme spent the previous three years turning perennial doormat Copperas Cove into a team to be reckoned with in Texas high school football's most competitive division, and Iowa Wesleyan was impressed with the turnaround he had orchestrated.

But when Mumme arrived at Iowa Wesleyan, he didn't bring the toolset that seemed to be standard issue for most football coaches trying to make their bones in the late 1980s. Mumme's plans to make the Tigers competitive on the football field didn't include a ball control offense that relied on a stingy defense. He wasn't carrying a playbook featuring the triple option that had been all the rage in major college football for nearly two decades. He didn't even have a playbook.

That's because in trying to capture Mumme's offense on paper, one quickly begins to feel like a dog chasing its own tail because simple X's and O's aren't quite adequate. Mumme's scheme was—and remains— a moving target, an offense constantly in flux, catering itself to the strengths and abilities of the players executing it. The crux of Mumme's offense was instilling an attitude in his coaching staff and his players, which was the aggressive pursuit of possibility based on an unwavering belief in one's self, no matter the odds or the situation.

Mumme's approach could be most easily described as an offensive scheme relying on the forward pass as its primary means of moving the ball. The offense stretched the field horizontally rather than vertically to deliver the ball to playmakers in space and trusted them to take advantage of the opportunities created by the geometrical paradigm shift. It was an approach that Mumme developed through extensive and ongoing film study of Brigham Young University's (BYU) wide open offense that made the Cougars a perpetual Top 25 contender and brought a national championship to Provo in 1984.

This was the same system Mumme ran with great success in his previous head coaching job at Copperas Cove High School (Texas), and people around the Lone Star State almost immediately began to take notice. Clyde Alexander, a veteran defensive coach and recruiter at Stephen F. Austin State University in Nacogdoches, Texas, told Mumme during a recruiting visit after his first season at Copperas Cove that his offense would change the way the Texas high school football was played. "You're going to change the face of this entire area in high school football," Alexander told him. "Every defense in this area will have to change because of what you did this year. Nobody expects Copperas Cove to score, much less win games."

Mumme figured that Alexander was trying to make his way into his good graces to gain an edge in recruiting, and he was probably right. But as the years have gone by, it's turned out that Alexander actually undersold the impact that Mumme's offense would have on the game. More than twenty years later, high schools across Texas and the entire United States run offenses that mimic or are inspired by the one ran at Copperas Cove from 1986 to 1988. But the schematic influence of Mumme's system does not end there.

Players and coaches who served key roles in orchestrating the gridiron success of Iowa Wesleyan from 1989 to 1991 have brought the principles of Mumme's offense to football programs all over the country. The nucleus of coaches from Iowa Wesleyan went to Georgia following the 1991 season when Mumme was hired as the head coach at Valdosta State University. After posting a 40–17–1 mark over five seasons at Valdosta State, Mumme took the head coaching job at Kentucky and debunked the myth that a team needed a power running game to compete in the rough-and-tumble Southeastern Conference (SEC) while rewriting the school's and the conference's offensive record books along the way.

From there, coaches from his staff began to branch out and take Mumme's offense with them. Iowa Wesleyan assistant coach Mike Leach brought the Texas Tech Red Raiders to ten consecutive bowl games and regularly beat Big 12 opponents such as Texas, Nebraska, and Oklahoma on the field, even though Texas Tech couldn't compete with those schools in recruiting talent.

Dana Holgorsen, a wide receiver at Iowa Wesleyan and a longtime assistant on Leach's staff at Texas Tech, went on to run offenses at Houston and Oklahoma State, which would lead the nation in total offense. In his first year as a head coach at West Virginia, Holgorsen won a conference title and set an Orange Bowl record for most points scored with the help of offensive line coach and former Iowa Wesleyan teammate Bill Bedenbaugh.

The offense's influence extends far beyond the coaches and players who were on hand for its inception. Mumme's rise to prominence and the success of those in his coaching tree have spawned similar schemes across the country at every level of play.

Mumme and his offense wound up doing a lot more than simply field a competitive football team at Iowa Wesleyan. In putting up prolific numbers on scoreboards and in box scores from 1989 to 1991, the Tigers and their offense, which would later come to be known as the Air Raid, weren't just winning football games; they were planting the seeds of college football's most prolific aerial revolution in the fertile Iowa soil beneath their feet in Mount Pleasant, Iowa.

1

THE JOURNEY
OF A THOUSAND MILES . . .

"Never take counsel of your fears." Thomas Jonathan "Stonewall" Jackson's famous quote on aggressive strategy was my mantra and is my best explanation for taking a huge cut in salary to move our family from Texas to Iowa. My belief in our offense and the opportunity to display it on the college level was the strategy.
—Hal Mumme

Yes, this is a book about football. Between its covers readers will find accounts of gridiron heroism achieved by unproven players under the direction of unproven coaches. It includes a comeback story that takes place so fast that it quickly becomes an afterthought within the arc of a greater narrative. Within that narrative there are anecdotes about the thinking man's game that takes place behind the scenes of a sport that many see as an exhibition of brute force. The entire book is basically an underdog story that continues to be written.

But it shouldn't be forgotten that this book also contains a love story. It's kind of scandalous, really, because in a lot of ways, the love story is something of an affair that involves a married man. As much as anything, this book is about Hal Mumme's rebuttal of conventional wisdom in favor of a love affair with offense—big, fast, sexy offense.

The offense in question put up numbers so big that many of the records that it established continue to stand to this day. It was an offense so fast that it took a football team from 0–10 to 7–3 in a single season. So sexy was this bombshell of an offense that nearly twenty-five years after the affair began, men across the country can't seem to keep their grubby mitts off of it and cries for the censorship of some of its racier elements have started to come from the Bible Belt.

Mumme consummated his love affair with offense in the summer of 1976 when he told his wife June that he would be leaving a promising job in his father's business to pursue his passion of football. When the conversation with his wife took place, Mumme had already accepted a position coaching quarterbacks and wide receivers at Moody High School in Corpus Christi, Texas. Coaching football was Mumme's new career path, and the matter was not open for discussion. The affair's revelation did not go over well at home.

When Mumme left his sales job, he and June already had a one-year-old son, Matt, to care for. The family needed security, and as far as June was concerned, coaching was an unreliable profession that required long hours and left one's job status subject to the performance of teenagers and the whims of irrational fan bases. She may have had a point. June was so infuriated by the news that she promptly went on strike from cooking for or speaking with Hal for three months.

Thanks to a strong assist from his wife's Catholic guilt, Mumme eventually made his way out of the doghouse, and as the years and jobs passed by, the Mumme family grew. A year or so into Mumme's new career in coaching, he and June had a daughter named Karen. Six years later, their second daughter Leslie was born. All the while, the family bounced around Texas following coaching jobs at the high school and collegiate level. As the Mumme family grew, so too did its patriarch's career. Mumme exhibited a knack for coaching at every stop he made in those early years, and he gradually progressed up the ranks of his chosen profession.

Along the way, the flames of Mumme's love for offense were fanned by a number of coaches, but few proved to be more influential than Don Davis, a fellow coach of Mumme's on Bill Yung's staff at West Texas State in Canyon, Texas. Davis recognized his colleague's talent and offered the following nugget of wisdom from his own coaching trials for the day when Mumme would become a head coach: it's easier to turn around a losing program if the fans believe the team can score lots of points.

For instance, when a defensive-minded coach loses a game 14–0, the circumstances somehow seem much bleaker. That's because the odds are that the coach is preaching worn-out clichés such as "offense wins games, but defense wins

6

championships" and the team is failing to deliver on both assertions. Meanwhile, no one enjoys watching the games because an evening full of three and outs are, objectively speaking, not any fun. An ineffective offense leaves the fan base feeling hopeless and when the coach crosses paths with fans they naturally ask, "What are you going to do to make this team competitive?" At this point the coach will regurgitate coach speak and more worn-out clichés about patience and progress because he can't blame losses on his players' inability to execute. Fans are alienated as the team continues to be represented by zeroes on the scoreboard. Meanwhile, the clock continues to tick on his inevitable firing.

On the other hand, if that same coach loses a game 42–28 it creates a completely different mentality. The kids will have fun scoring points and fans will enjoy coming to the games because an evening full of 40-yard touchdown passes are, objectively speaking, lots of fun. When that same coach crosses paths with the fans they naturally say, "Boy, that was an exciting game on Friday night!"

At this point the coach will respond with something to the effect of, "I know, we almost had 'em, didn't we?"

"We sure did," random fan will say as he nods in agreement. "Now, if you could only find a defensive coordinator."

Davis's insight was so comprehensive that he even offered a suggestion as to which offense Mumme should run. "I never change the channel when BYU is playing on TV." In the late 1970s and early 1980s LaVell Edwards' prolific pass-first offense brought shares of ten consecutive Western Athletic Conference (WAC) titles to Provo, making the Cougars the nation's most entertaining football team in the process. It was settled; Mumme would run BYU's offense when he became a head coach, and that's exactly what he did when he landed the head coaching job at Copperas Cove High School in 1986.

In the years since I left Copperas Cove High School, the football program has gone on to become a perennial winner under the guidance of head coach Jack Welch who has truly worked magic there for the past twenty seasons. In that time, he's coached a number of players who have gone onto the NFL, including Robert Griffin III. Jack was an assistant coach along with me at West Texas State University and was also greatly influenced by Don Davis and Bill Yung.

Before Mumme's arrival at the central Texas high school, Copperas Cove was a perennial doormat, winning only fourteen games in the previous twelve seasons. In three years at the helm, Mumme's teams won twelve games on the wings of its high-flying offense and reignited the community's enthusiasm for high school football in the process. Davis's words had been prophetic, and Mumme was anxious to try out his approach to the game at the college level. The opportunity that would return him to the college game came on New Year's Day 1989.

Mumme was at home watching the Rose Bowl when received a call from Dr. Robert Prins, President of Iowa Wesleyan College in Mount Pleasant, Iowa. Prins and Mumme had a mutual friend in Steve Kazor, a special teams coach with the Chicago Bears. It was Kazor who suggested that Mumme apply for the opportunity in the first place, and it was Kazor who told Prins that he'd be a fool not to hire a man who could make Copperas Cove believe in its high school football team. Mumme had originally interviewed for the job in December and was quickly offered the position, but the initial salary proposal didn't meet the needs of his family. After Iowa Wesleyan's administration scrambled in vain to find another candidate who could inspire something resembling hope in their comatose football program, they improved their offer and Mumme accepted. The new salary still represented a drastic pay cut for Mumme, but it was a number that he felt his family could manage and besides, the job would deliver him back into the college game.

Then came the hard part: Mumme had to explain to his thirteen-year-old son and his twelve-year-old daughter that the family was moving to Iowa. In the past thirteen years the family had moved all over Texas and Matt was beginning to draw great pride from his home state, as Texans tend to do. Karen was in middle school and her friends had become the center of her universe. Their youngest, Leslie, was only five at the time, so it was reasonable to think that she was still too young to really grasp the implications of the move. Mumme and June knew that this was going to be the first of the family's half-dozen relocation efforts that would inspire real anguish in any of their children.

As per the family ritual when a new job and moving were on the horizon, Mumme called a family meeting. Matt and Karen, seasoned veterans of what had become a game of Texas hop scotch, entered the living room in timid fashion. They knew what family meetings meant, and they regarded them with the type of suspicion, fear, and disdain usually reserved for terminally ill patients awaiting a doctor's prognosis. Mumme sat his family in a circle and began by saying, "Guys, you know I love you, but sometimes in life you have to do things that you don't want to do and now is one of those times. We're moving to Iowa." Before he could go any further he was promptly interrupted by Karen bursting into tears. After a moment she sprung up from her seat in the living room and sprinted to her bedroom.

Matt began to panic, but fell back on his recent lessons on Lone Star State geography in an effort to calm himself down. "Iowa, Texas . . . Iowa, Texas . . . where in Texas is Iowa?" he thought to himself. As he continued to grasp for a straw that didn't exist he finally asked, "Dad, where is Iowa, Texas?"

"No, not Iowa, Texas," the elder Mumme explained to his son. "We're moving to a state called *Iowa*." The revelation sent Matt's efforts to ward off the panic created by the impending move directly into the toilet. He got up and retired to his room to digest the bombshell and perform emotional damage control in a more isolated setting. Shunned by their two oldest children, the Mummes looked down to find five-year-old Leslie sitting on the floor following her older siblings' lead, bawling her little blue eyes out. The emotional bomb strike was complete, and nothing was left to do but begin triage.

As is the case with most middle school girls, the notion of leaving her friends left Karen inconsolable. There was little the Mummes could say or do to make the situation feel like any less of a death sentence for their oldest daughter. Hal and June did their best to lift Matt's spirits by trying to get him to focus on the positive aspects of moving to Iowa. They told him that all of his new classmates would want to be his friend; his father would be the football coach in town and he would have a cool, exotic Texas accent. Matt was still weary of this state called Iowa, but he did his best to buy what his parents were selling. Cheering up Leslie proved to be a much easier endeavor. It turned out she was afraid that she wasn't going to be able to bring her toys or her hamster with her to Iowa. When she learned that both would be making the journey with the family, Leslie quickly came around on the idea of living in the Hawkeye State.

Although the children's reactions may have been dramatic, they weren't completely without basis. The Iowa Wesleyan experiment got underway a few weeks later when the Mummes packed into a red Ford Aerostar and made the nearly thousand-mile journey from their home in central Texas to southeast Iowa. After stopping in Kansas City for the night, the Mummes completed the journey to Mount Pleasant the following morning and began to move their belongings into a rental house that had been recommended by the school's administration. The Mummes had only seen the house in a fax sent by Iowa Wesleyan's athletic director David Johnsen. When they laid eyes on the house for the first time, it turned out there was quite a bit that didn't translate in the grainy black-and-white photographs that they had received through their fax machine.

9

Having a great athletic director is essential for a winning football program. Iowa Wesleyan had David Johnsen. New to the job, David had previously been the football team's defensive coordinator; he became a great supporter and even filled in as a position coach during our first season when we were understaffed. Most importantly, he had a vision that Iowa Wesleyan could win.

The outside of the house was covered by an ancient layer of crumbling paint and frilly, antiquated woodwork from a bygone era. "It was basically the Victorian version of the Addams Family house," Mumme recalled of his introduction to the family's first residence in Mount Pleasant. Walking through the front door offered little reprieve from the horror of its exterior. The walls, ceilings, and floors shared the state of neglect found on the outside of the house. Hideous wallpaper peeled from the walls. Because the house was a bit larger than the foundation, frost had accumulated in the corners of several rooms. The only full bathroom on the second floor felt like a closet with a toilet and a shower, and initial attempts at bathing resulted in significant leakage into the room below.

As the day eased into evening and as the Mummes tried to get some sleep after a long day of travel and unpacking, their attempts at peaceful slumber were interrupted by an unexpected squatter that flew out of the chimney to terrorize the home's new residents. As the bat flew around the house, most of the family ducked for cover in their bedrooms while Mumme grabbed a tennis racket and prepared for battle. He stalked the bat throughout the first floor with the fury of Inigo Montoya, and after a couple of whiffs, he finally delivered a forehand that sent the winged intruder spiraling into the fireplace, meeting the bricks with a vicious thud.

Mentally and physically exhausted from a day full of travel, disappointment, and uninvited winged beasts, Mumme disposed of the carcass and laid down in bed to get some rest before he began his first day on the job. He came to Mount Pleasant with the idyllic notion that he would spend the rest of his life coaching at Iowa Wesleyan, walking across campus to work each day, and becoming a fixture in the community. In less than twelve hours, that vision was destroyed. As he drifted off to sleep, Mumme's head was dominated by a single thought: "I've got to win some games and get my family the hell out of here."

2

REBUILDING A PROGRAM

"I remember it like it was yesterday," recalls Mumme of his first day on Iowa Wesleyan's campus in late January 1989. "It was the bleakest place I'd ever seen." There was two feet of snow on the ground. Everything was dead. Iowa Wesleyan's 550-member student body made its way to and from class in frigid silence. And the football team that Mumme had been hired to coach didn't even exist. Well, it existed in theory. Iowa Wesleyan had a ninety-two-year tradition on the gridiron, complete with a mascot, uniforms, a home field, and a schedule to play come autumn. It just didn't have enough players to actually field a team.

During his first day on Iowa Wesleyan's campus, Mumme attended two meetings. The first was a press conference to introduce him as the new head football coach at the small National Association of Intercollegiate Athletics (NAIA) school to which all of two reporters showed up to cover. The attendance for the second gathering of the day, a team meeting that Mumme called to get acquainted with the Tigers' returning players, didn't fare much better. Only eight players showed up, and three of those eight were only on campus because they followed Mumme from his previous job as head football coach at Copperas Cove.

The other attendees were the only five players whose egos managed to survive the attrition of Iowa Wesleyan's winless 1988 campaign. The Tigers' 0–10 record the season prior combined with a 76–316 point differential in those losses had created an epidemic lack of morale among its players. To make matters worse, Mumme managed to sufficiently alienate four of the remaining five members

11

of the '88 squad during the meeting when he mentioned a mandatory offseason strength-and-conditioning program, leaving the rebuilding football program with only four players on its roster.

After the team meeting, Mumme sat down at the desk he shared with the women's basketball coach in Iowa Wesleyan's athletic office to assess the gloomy state of affairs. Joining him was his defensive coordinator and the only assistant coach at the moment, Mike Major. Major had been an assistant to Mumme during the previous three seasons at Copperas Cove, and the two of them had worked together at Mumme's first job coaching quarterbacks and wide receivers at Moody High School. The pair was later reunited at on Bill Yung's coaching staff at University of Texas El Paso in the early 1980s.

During their time as colleagues, Mumme and Major built a strong rapport with one another on and off the football field. They spent a number of late nights in the kitchen at the Mumme household watching reels of 16-mm game film projected onto the refrigerator door, usually after Major had enjoyed dinner with the rest of the family. Eventually, the duo kicked their film study up a notch when they began making annual trips to Provo, Utah, to pore through the video library of the football team at BYU.

Thanks to their familiarity with one another, the conversation didn't last long. There was a brief moment of silence between the two before Major shook his head and blurted out, "I don't know about you, but I'm going recruiting." Not long after, he began the 250-mile trek east to Chicago to begin his efforts to find bodies to fill out Iowa Wesleyan's roster. This left Mumme behind to fill out the coaching staff, find some local talent, and drum up support for the program around the Mount Pleasant community. With that, Mumme and Major got to work resurrecting the football program at Iowa Wesleyan.

If nothing else, Mumme's early efforts to assemble a coaching staff proved to be an amusing endeavor. Before his brief strategy session with Major, Mumme found dozens of pink message notes littering his desk. As it turned out, the Tiger football program's futility was a poorly kept secret throughout the Midwest. All but two of the fifty or so messages scrawled on the notes covering his desk came from athletic directors looking to schedule their homecoming games with Iowa Wesleyan.

The first message that wasn't seeking a patsy to throw on its schedule came from someone out in Los Angeles who may or may have not have had gang affiliations. He offered to bring a bunch of "his guys" to Mount Pleasant to play football, provided that Mumme would find a spot for him on the coaching staff.

The second message was from an aspiring football coach, who spent the previous season coaching defensive ends at College of the Desert, by the name of Mike Leach.

Leach's coaching resume was unorthodox to say the least. After graduating from BYU where he had not played football, he earned a law degree at Pepperdine University where he learned, among other things, that the law was not his life's calling. From there Leach went to the US Sports Academy in Alabama where he got a master's degree in sports science. This was followed by a stint as a volunteer assistant coach at Cal Poly–San Luis Obispo before coaching at College of the Desert.

What Leach's credentials lacked in traditional experience he made up for with enthusiasm, intelligence, and a proclivity to work for a salary that hovered around the poverty line. Furthermore, Leach's unconventional coaching background proved to be a desirable quality thanks to his readiness to accept the less traditional aspects of the offense Mumme planned to install at Iowa Wesleyan, particularly on the offensive line where Mumme planned to have Leach coach.

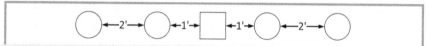

Typical offensive line alignment in 1989, with the linemen in tight splits (between one and two feet apart) and a three-point stance.

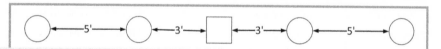

Iowa Wesleyan's offensive line alignment, with the linemen in wide splits (between three and five feet apart) and a two-point stance.

Mumme believed in setting up his offensive line in two point stances with wide splits between them, which were two fairly revolutionary concepts at the time. Veteran offensive line coaches were reluctant to set their players up in this fashion because their experience allowed them only to see the potential pitfalls of this approach, which was the supposed ease with which defensive lineman could run through those wider gaps. However, wider gaps also created larger passing lanes and put greater distance between the quarterback and the opposing team's best pass rusher, the defensive end. The two-point stance allowed offensive lineman to survey the field more easily and put them in a position that left them better prepared to pass block. Leach's inexperience came along with a willingness to embrace the possibilities that Mumme's beliefs regarding offensive line play presented rather than rely on his experience as a rationalization for his fears.

After Mumme's first few phone conversations with Leach, he knew that he would hire Leach. Nevertheless, Leach was unyielding in establishing a relationship with Iowa Wesleyan's new head football coach. "Mike would wear me out on the phone at night," remembered Mumme. The two of them would spend hours discussing the finer points of Mumme's unique offensive philosophy and how they translated to the offensive line.

During the first week of April, Mumme and Leach met face-to-face for the first time in Provo during BYU's spring football practice to watch film of the Cougars' pass-oriented offense. During their time on BYU's campus, Mumme conducted an informal interview in which Leach secured the job. "Just meeting Mike, you knew he could do anything he wanted," Mumme said of their first face-to-face meeting. Although Mumme knew that he would hire Leach within their first few phone calls, the trip afforded them the opportunity to get to know one another on a personal level. The trip also gave Leach a chance to see what Mumme's offense would look like in action.

Although Mumme's trip to Provo helped to hone his schematic approach and shore up his coaching staff, his time there also delivered a personal victory on the home front. One afternoon, he got word that there was a call for him from his wife back in Mount Pleasant. Fearing an emergency with one of the kids, Mumme raced to the phone to find out why June was calling. When he answered the phone, June informed Mumme that she had bought a house. Although the previous owner's penchant for the color orange created an ambience that left one feeling as if they were living inside of a jack-o-lantern, the rest of it was absolutely charming and only minor renovations were required to make the house a home. The beautiful Victorian home was more than one hundred years old but represented a stark improvement from the rental house the Mummes had been living in for the past couple of months.

Mumme returned home at the end of the week and began preparing to move his family into a residence that felt like a return to civilized society. A month later, Leach came to campus and Iowa Wesleyan's administration signed off on his hiring as long as he agreed to serve as sports information director, equipment manager, and teach a few law classes on campus. As spring began to ease into summer, Mumme's personal and professional life in Mount Pleasant looked to be on the upswing.

Beyond the hiring of Major and Leach, Iowa Wesleyan provided Mumme with a $10,000 budget to compensate the rest of his coaching staff. This money was meant to be spread around to all of the coaches that would be working with the football team as a small incentive for coaching the entire year in what was essentially a volunteer role. However, Mumme figured that if someone was willing to coach for $2,000, they were probably willing to coach for free, so he used the entirety of that allotment to hire a coach who would address the Tigers' greatest need: strength and conditioning.

Mumme knew that recruiting an entire roster in six months would monopolize most of the coaching staff's waking hours, leaving them with little or no time to run the type of workouts that would prepare the players who were already on campus for a season of college football. Therefore, finding someone to ensure those players were working hard to prepare for the season became a priority. Dan Wirth proved to be the ideal candidate to whip the ragtag roster, which the coaching staff was assembling, into fighting shape. Wirth played his college football at University of Iowa before pursuing a master's degree in Exercise and Sports Science and serving as a graduate assistant on legendary football coach Hayden Fry's coaching staff at his alma mater.

In addition to Wirth's hiring, Mumme's staff also came to include a couple holdovers from the previous coaching regime. Iowa Wesleyan's athletic director David Johnsen was retained to coach the wide receivers. Mumme also kept on Eric Prins as defensive line coach, who was also the women's basketball coach and the son of college president Dr. Robert Prins, thereby fulfilling an unwritten nepotism clause in Mumme's contract.

Running backs coach Marshall Cotton grew up in Davenport, Iowa, and played his college football with the Iowa Hawkeyes. Kirk Soukup, an alumnus of the Iowa Wesleyan football program and a first-team All-American in 1983, was hired to coach defensive backs. Assistant defensive coach Dean Hamilton rounded out the Tiger coaching staff.

As he went through the process of recruiting players and hiring a coaching staff, Mumme simultaneously worked to gain the support of as many of Mount Pleasant's ten thousand residents as possible. Those efforts were carried out per the instructions of Don Davis, Mumme's former colleague on the staff at West Texas State. Davis had once advised Mumme to join the town's decision makers for morning coffee when he became a head coach. "You're the football coach in town, they're going to talk about you anyway," Davis told him. "You may as well be there to defend yourself."

In Mount Pleasant, that place was Dicky's Maid-Rite, an amalgamation gas station, sandwich shop, and convenience store. The specialty at Dicky's was the maid rite sandwich—a gratuitous and polarizing meaty confection that the town's residents revered and detested with equal fervor—and heated conversation. Mumme quickly made morning coffee at Dicky's a staple of his daily routine.

However, early on, Mumme had little defending to do. Thanks to the team's uninspired performance in the seasons that preceded his hiring, Tiger football was rarely a topic of discussion at Dicky's. The regulars were much more interested in discussing Fry's Iowa Hawkeyes or taking sides in the ongoing blood feud in the National League East between the Chicago Cubs and St. Louis Cardinals. Nonetheless, Mumme continued to frequent Dicky's, offering his thoughts on Hawkeye football, choosing a side in the Cubs–Cardinals fracas (despite being a Texas Rangers fan his entire adult life), and getting familiar with some of the more influential members of the Mount Pleasant community. Few, if any, would ultimately prove to be a stronger advocate for Mumme's fledgling program than the operator of Dicky's Maid-Rite, Bob Lamm.

Lamm was born and raised in Mount Pleasant and had been front and center for the gradual decline of Iowa Wesleyan's football team over the past four seasons. "It wasn't much of a program," recalled Lamm as he conjured images of team conditioning sessions featuring haggard equipment and minimal enthusiasm that led to being on the wrong side of 52–0 outcomes come game day. Only a few days into Mumme's tenure as football coach Lamm headed to Iowa Wesleyan's athletic offices to introduce himself to the new coach and deliver the following message: "I don't have any money, but I know all the people that do." He went on to say that he was happy to help the new coach in any way that he could and introduce him to anyone in town who could help the football program. Mumme was happy to make his acquaintance.

The following week, Lamm brought Mumme as his guest to a Chamber of Commerce function to generate interest in the rebuilding program and help the new coach make some valuable connections within the community. While the pair was en route, Mumme told Lamm that he intended to raise $25,000 for the program before the season. It was an aggressive figure for a football team that didn't even bother charging admission for its own poorly attended home games, but Lamm politely nodded, rolled his eyes, and thought to himself, "This guy's crazy."

By his own admission, Lamm was by no means the wealthiest member of the Mount Pleasant community, but he exerted as much influence as anyone in town.

He found himself in the middle of most of the important decisions being made in Mount Pleasant because people found him trustworthy and they valued his opinion. This was probably because Lamm had no reservations about giving his honest and unfiltered opinion. In a small town like Mount Pleasant, someone willing to deliver the unvarnished truth was a complete anomaly because most people were busy trying to be polite. Presented with the option of being honest or accommodating, most residents would forgo delivering their frank opinion in favor of being polite to preserve the harmony of their relationship and the community. The odds were pretty good that they'd be running into each other tomorrow after all. Few new people ever came to Mount Pleasant to stay, and even fewer people ever left. Lamm was one of a handful of people in town who could be counted on to say something was a bad idea, and somehow he got away with it. It also didn't hurt that he just so happened to be around for virtually all of the important discussions because they were taking place at Dicky's.

Those decisions included lots of small-town matters such as where to place the crosswalks on the town square when it was shut down for the Easter Egg Hunt in March, or which local teenagers would be asked to detassel corn come July. (Detasseling, an important step in corn cultivation that involves removing the tassels from the top of a corn stalk and placing them on the ground to promote cross-pollination and improve crop yield, was a rite of passage in many farming communities in Iowa as well as throughout the Midwest. Mount Pleasant was no exception. Detasseling provided local adolescents with an opportunity to earn good money and learn the value of a hard day's work through one of the more miserable tasks agriculture has to offer.)

Thanks to Mumme's stable presence at Dicky's and his willingness to offer his (or his players') assistance with a variety of odd jobs throughout town, John Lance, a local surveyor and head of the Iowa Wesleyan Booster Club, asked Mumme's fourteen-year old son Matt to be a part of the community's detasseling efforts in the spring. Matt's detasseling career lasted all of ten minutes before he got to thinking, "There's got to be better stuff to do than this," and took off to find a part-time job that didn't require him to spend twelve repetitive and tedious hours a day in a cornfield. Although the younger Mumme's detassling career lasted less than a day before he called it quits, having him chosen to join the effort was a nice nod of approval from the community toward the efforts of Iowa Wesleyan's new head football coach before his team had even played a snap.

17

By morning, Mumme was at Dicky's drinking coffee and earning the support of the Mount Pleasant community for his fledgling football program. By afternoon he was making his way around Iowa recruiting players to supplement the efforts of Major, who was out scouring the rest of Middle America for overlooked talent. One of the first players Mumme went to visit was a highly regarded prospect out of Mount Pleasant High School by the name of Dana Holgorsen. Not only was Holgorsen a talented wide receiver, but he was also the type of local product that the Mount Pleasant community would want to come out and support come fall, which would hopefully provide a worthwhile incentive for people to actually pay for a ticket at Mapleleaf Field.

When Mumme arrived on campus at Mount Pleasant High School, he made his way to the administrative offices and asked to see Bob Evans. Evans was the school's principal, resident football coaching legend, and a fellow member of the Dicky's morning coffee crowd with whom Mumme had built a good rapport. While Mumme and Evans stuck around the office and talked football, an aide was sent to Holgorsen's English class to inform him that Iowa Wesleyan's head coach was there to see him. Unfortunately for Mumme, his interest in Holgorsen was not reciprocated.

Holgorsen sent the office aide back to the principal's office alone, telling the aide that he'd rather stick out the next thirty minutes in class than bother talking with Iowa Wesleyan's new head coach. He was already committed to follow his older brother to play football at St. Ambrose University in Davenport, Iowa, and he was anxious to make his way to the big city of ninety-five thousand. The first seventeen years of his life had been spent in the sleepy town, and he had no interest in spending the next four there as well. Furthermore, if he was going to spend his time spinning his wheels with a football coach, it certainly wouldn't be Iowa Wesleyan's.

Holgorsen's complete void of interest in joining the football program at Iowa Wesleyan turned out to be a fair representation of the mind-set of most recruits who lived close enough to Mount Pleasant to actually be familiar with Iowa Wesleyan's football team. Clearly, Mumme was going to have to look elsewhere to find the type of talent he needed to win.

Fortunately, he came from central Texas, where high school football talent abounded. After a number of unsuccessful recruiting visits in southeast Iowa, Mumme decided that he needed some help, so he called on players Bob Draper and Dennis Gatewood, who had come with him from Copperas Cove. He was hoping to have a brainstorming session to come up with talented opponents from their district that weren't playing college football but might be interested in

18

doing so at Iowa Wesleyan. To supplement their brainstorming efforts, Mumme flew in their former teammate and all-district quarterback from Copperas Cove, Dustin Dewald. In addition to assisting in the search for capable players to help the Tigers on the gridiron, Mumme was hoping that Dewald would choose to join the team himself.

Great quarterbacks have a passion for the game as we play it. I knew Dustin Dewald had that passion in him. It's interesting how style of play can affect and literally overwhelm players, especially quarterbacks. Dustin not only loved our style of play, he also had all the intangibles a quarterback needs to win.

Dewald's college career began at Stephen F. Austin State University in Nacogdoches, Texas, where he was recruited to play football. He saw action in four games during his freshman year before he found himself burnt out by the game, so he hung up his football cleats with plans to transfer to Tarleton State University in Stephenville, Texas, and play golf. Despite his apparent lack of interest in continuing his football career, bringing Dewald to Mount Pleasant became Mumme's first priority when he was named head coach at Iowa Wesleyan. The recruitment of Dewald began shortly after Mumme accepted the position. Dewald was home from college on Christmas break when the news of Mumme's hiring at Iowa Wesleyan began to spread around Copperas Cove, so Dewald headed to Mumme's office to congratulate him. It was then that Mumme first posed the question, "How would you like to move to Iowa?" Dewald, a twenty-year-old newlywed at the time, exhibited maturity beyond his years with his response. "Let me talk to Tiff," Dewald replied, and headed home to discuss the potential move with his wife.

Fortunately for Dewald and Mumme, Tiffany was on board for the move to Iowa. She enjoyed moving around and experiencing new places, and going with her husband to Mount Pleasant presented just such an opportunity. From Dewald's perspective, following his high school coach to Iowa presented an opportunity to make football fun again. Going to Iowa Wesleyan would reunite Dewald with a number of his former high school teammates and friends from Copperas Cove who had already signed on to become Tigers. It also didn't hurt that in Mumme's system he would be given free reign over an offense that started throwing the ball as soon as it got off the bus.

As quarterback, Dewald would be the focal point of the Tiger's pass-oriented attack, a system that he was already familiar with thanks to his time directing Mumme's offense at Copperas Cove. Experience with the offense wasn't the only quality Dewald brought to the table. Despite his fairly quiet demeanor and a rather unassuming physical presence at 6 feet and 175 pounds, Dewald was the type of mature, confident leader that a team of people who were essentially strangers would naturally gravitate toward and follow through adversity. In bringing him aboard, Mumme put the centerpiece of the Tigers' roster into place.

On the other side of the ball, Mumme found a defensive leader in Randy Perez, a free safety out of Ranger Junior College in Ranger, Texas. Mumme and his former players were familiar with Perez from competing against him while they were at Copperas Cove. Perez, who played his prep football at Round Rock High School outside of Austin, was a galvanizing defensive presence who had a football savvy about him that he inherited from his father Ines, who was also Randy's high school coach. The elder Perez was also a highly regarded football player for Fry at Southern Methodist University (SMU) before becoming a respected high school coach in Texas.

Ines was SMU's second string quarterback in 1967 when the Mustangs started their season with a nationally televised game against Texas A&M. At the start of the second half, the starter left the game with an injury; Ines was inserted into the lineup and completed 10 of 12 passes for 117 yards, including a six-yard touchdown pass to Jerry Levias with four seconds remaining. The performance delivered a memorable 20–17 victory for the Mustangs. After the game, a joyful Fry called Levias and the five-foot, four-inch Perez "my two little giants."

Between Dewald, Perez, and a number of other former players and opponents, Mumme and Major were having tremendous success recruiting their home state. It wasn't difficult selling his program to players who were familiar with his teams at Copperas Cove, because in many ways those players were already sold on Mumme, or at least what they knew his offense was capable of. However, it became apparent that the coaching staff would need to be successful recruiting elsewhere if they were going to assemble a complete, let alone a competitive, roster.

Unsure of the lengths he was allowed to go to in selling recruits on Iowa Wesleyan, Mumme consulted the NAIA rulebook. When it comes to recruiting, the NAIA bylaws include only thirty-three ambiguous words that essentially stipulate that competing institutions can do anything in the recruitment of athletes that they would do to recruit an otherwise gifted prospective student: "All student recruiting for athletic purposes shall be in harmony with recommended and acceptable practices of the institution and shall be controlled by the regularly constituted institutional committee on student loans and scholarships."

Unclear on Iowa Wesleyan's common recruitment practices for talented students, Mumme went to see Dr. Mildred Bensmiller, a professor of concert piano who had recruited a number of world class pianists over the years to come to Mount Pleasant and study under her tutelage. His primary interest was to learn whether or not she used paid visits in her recruitment of pianists because the standard set by Dr. Bensmiller would dictate what Iowa Wesleyan's coaching staff would be allowed to do in their pursuit of talented football players. On learning that Dr. Bensmiller did in fact provide for paid visits to recruit students to Iowa Wesleyan, Mumme was overjoyed. "Dr. B, you did me a great favor, I appreciate it!" he exclaimed before racing out of her office to launch one of the more aggressive recruiting efforts that Iowa Wesleyan's football program had ever seen.

Mount Pleasant resident John Wright was one of the biggest employers in the state of Iowa, owned his own airplane, and was a member of Iowa Wesleyan's booster club. He quickly became the most important figure in Iowa Wesleyan's recruiting efforts who wasn't a member of the coaching staff. After some bargaining, Wright agreed to let Mumme send his plane to pick up recruits and bring them to Iowa Wesleyan's campus when he didn't need it for business purposes.

Offensive linemen John Coneset and Andrew Przybylski were among the talented prep athletes who were impressed with the lengths Iowa Wesleyan showed itself willing to go to in securing their services on the gridiron. Both players spent the past two years anchoring Chicago-area Joliet Junior College's offensive line at center and guard, respectively. Each possessed the strength and skill set of National Collegiate Athletic Association (NCAA) Division I linemen, but they lacked the necessary height to be scholarship material. Major, who had taken the lead in recruiting the pair of talented linemen, may have stalled his pursuit of their services had it not been for a key discovery that he made during the recruitment process.

Tom Horne, the Wolves' third year head coach, had taken the helm at Joliet two years after delivering an 8–3 season at Iowa Wesleyan in 1984. Despite the success that he found in Mount Pleasant, Horne was run off by the college's administration for philosophical differences pertaining to the direction of the football program. After a year in coaching purgatory, the spurned head coach brought several former Tigers along with him to Joliet as coaches, including his offensive line coach who had built a strong relationship with Coneset and Przybylski in their two years with the Wolves.

21

After connecting these dots, Major began making the hard sell to the coaching staff's nostalgic inclinations to direct Coneset and Przybylski to the Tigers. Although his split with Iowa Wesleyan had been acrimonious, Horne was impressed with the effort the new coaching staff was making to bring talent back to Mount Pleasant and ultimately gave his blessing to Major and Iowa Wesleyan.

The endorsement of Joliet's coaching staff combined with the impression left by Wright's plane was enough to bring Coneset and Przybylski to Mount Pleasant to play for the Tigers. It proved to be a winning formula for many other talented players across the country that had somehow slipped through the cracks of NCAA recruitment as well.

When the dust settled on the rest of Iowa Wesleyan's recruiting efforts, the hard work of Major, Mumme, their former high school players, and the rest of the coaching staff yielded a roster of sixty-three, thirty-two of which hailed from the Lone Star State. Six members of the team came from Iowa, which was fewer than Mumme, his fellow coaches, and the administration had initially hoped. Regarding the difficulty they had attracting local talent in 1989, Mumme commented to a local reporter, "It seems that those closest to you see your problems instead of your good points." Outside of Iowa, players had far fewer preconceived notions about Iowa Wesleyan football, and it wasn't nearly as difficult to sell recruits on the Tigers' upside. In addition to the thirty-two players from Texas, Illinois, Kansas, and Missouri were well represented on the roster thanks to Wright's private plane and Major's nomadic endeavors.

Major began his 1989 recruiting tour by driving 250 miles east to Chicago and then meandering his way down to Houston, stopping to meet recruits and selling them on the opportunity to join something special at Iowa Wesleyan along the way. Life on the road would soon take a considerable toll on Major's health as he began to develop ulcers in his stomach about a month into recruiting season. By May, things got so bad he had to check himself into a hospital to have nearly a third of his stomach cut out to remove the ulcers. Unfazed, he returned to the recruiting trail almost immediately, joining Mumme on a trip to east Texas days after his procedure. The two drove from town to town, recruiting new players and checking in on signees to make sure they still intended to report to Mount Pleasant for football camp in August. Every hundred miles or so, the two of them would have to pull over for Major to get out of the car and vomit, the result of a chronic upset stomach he was dealing with in the aftermath of his procedure.

Major's sacrifices did not go unrewarded. His efforts delivered the majority of the sixty-three players who would participate in Iowa Wesleyan's preseason camp come August. In addition to recruits, Major and his car also racked up a $3,500 mileage bill for the college to reimburse. Sensing the recruiting efforts of their new coaching staff would be more aggressive and far-reaching than those of the past, the administration saw to it that Major received a courtesy car so they could avoid receiving similar invoices in the future.

Major's courtesy car wasn't the only upgrade that the football program received from the administration that offseason. In the summer of 1989, the coaching staff moved into remodeled offices and the players began working out in a new weight room on campus. Iowa Wesleyan's booster club supplemented the administration's efforts to upgrade the team's facilities by volunteering their time to put up a new fence around the team's practice field. Mumme was impressed with the support the Mount Pleasant community was showing his football team. Leading up to the season he commented to a local reporter, "These people are really behind us. They are making the kids feel at home and are letting them know they want these kids to win football games. We wouldn't have all these new players here if it wasn't for the people of this town and their kindness."

With the 1989 football season looming, the hours spent behind the wheel, sitting at kitchen tables with the families of recruits, and drinking coffee in Dicky's Maid-Rite were paying off. From exceptionally uncertain beginnings, Mumme had managed to put together a coaching staff, fill out the roster, and rally community support for Iowa Wesleyan's football program. The key ingredients for a successful season were present. With the arrival of their first football camp in Mount Pleasant, the time had come for Mumme and the rest of his coaching staff to bring them all together.

3

A TEAM COMES TOGETHER

On a cold February morning, somewhere along the forty-three-mile stretch of highway between Iowa City and Mount Pleasant, Dan Wirth nearly lost his drive. At the time Wirth was headed to Mount Pleasant to meet Hal Mumme about Iowa Wesleyan's vacant strength coaching position, and for at least a few moments, he wasn't sure if he was up to the challenges presented by the new role. Becoming the Tigers' strength coach would require Wirth, a twenty-three-year-old graduate assistant on Hayden Fry's coaching staff at University of Iowa, to give up his position with the Hawkeyes and make the one-hundred-mile round trip between Iowa City and Mount Pleasant a daily ritual.

He first heard of the opportunity a few days previously when an assistant coach at Iowa asked if Wirth would consider the possibility of becoming the head strength coach at a small college instead of continuing with limited responsibility in his graduate assistant role at the Big 10 powerhouse. On being presented with the idea, the chance to run his own strength program outweighed the burden of piling a two-hour daily commute and a full-time strength coaching gig on top of his graduate studies. "Anything I can do to start running my own program would be great," Wirth thought. So he agreed to meet with Iowa Wesleyan's head coach about the possibility of joining the Tiger coaching staff the following week.

On the day he was to meet with Mumme, Wirth got into his car and began driving to Mount Pleasant. As the wheels and the odometer continued to roll, the burden of a long commute, greater coaching responsibility, and his studies began to weigh heavier. Eventually, feeling overwhelmed, he pulled over to the side of Route 27's southbound lane and took a moment to indulge the thought that had been creeping to the front of his mind since he began driving: "I don't think I can do this."

As the minutes passed and cars whizzed by, he sat behind the wheel of his stationary car, and another thought crept into his head. "I've made it this far," Wirth figured, "I don't want to stand the guy up." So he pulled back onto the road and kept on driving to Dicky's Maid-Rite for his interview, compelled by decency rather than enthusiasm.

When finally he arrived at Dicky's and actually sat down with Mumme, Wirth found his enthusiasm restored. Mumme wasted no time explaining the role he hoped his strength coach would play in Iowa Wesleyan's gridiron revival. He wanted a strength coach who could be a steady presence for the players and keep the lines of communication between the team and the coaching staff open throughout the offseason. While the rest of the coaching staff was on the road recruiting, Wirth would be the one to keep the players focused on their personal goals and improving each day leading up to their first game. At the time, having a full-time coach to serve in such a capacity was a fairly innovative concept, especially for a school the size of Iowa Wesleyan.

Wirth responded to Mumme's expectations by sharing his approach to strength training, which began with accepting nothing less than 100 percent effort in every workout session from each member of the team. Wirth went on to share his experiences and his vision for training before Mumme was able to address the biggest setback to Iowa Wesleyan's proposed strength program. When Wirth finished, Mumme expressed his satisfaction with Wirth's training philosophies before he dropped a bomb. "Well, the only problem is we don't have a weight room."

Little more than an hour ago, the reality of a two-hour daily commute left Wirth on the side of the road, contemplating a U-turn back to Iowa City. This setback, a complete void of a functional weight room or adequate training facilities, left Wirth unfazed and he agreed to come aboard before he even had the opportunity to meet the rest of the coaching staff. "Because of Hal's enthusiasm, I decided to do this," he later said of his decision to join the rebuilding effort at Iowa Wesleyan.

Wirth's first order of business on the job was remedying Iowa Wesleyan's weight room problem. After his initial interview at Dicky's, Mumme brought Wirth to campus to show him the basement of McKibben Hall, the only men's dormitory on campus. The basement was essentially a large open space that was being used for storage at the time. The effort required to transform the muddled basement into a functional workout area ended up providing some of the first workouts for the few players who were actually on campus. Early conditioning sessions consisted of Wirth getting the team together to haul away the junk cluttering the basement floor so that they would have an open space to work out in during the cold Iowa winter.

Although the basement of McKibben Hall provided protection from the elements, the team's efforts did little to eliminate the consequences of poor design and years of neglect. The floor was little more than a moist sand pit and there was a sewer leak coming from the ceiling that ensured the basement always smelled like a neglected Porta Potty. The ambience of outright filth was complimented nicely by a pile of junk in the corner that had yet to be hauled to the campus's overflowing dumpsters.

Despite their less than sanitary surroundings, every afternoon throughout spring semester, Iowa Wesleyan's players proved their mettle by descending into the dungeon for strength-and-conditioning sessions with Wirth. Despite the bootleg and somewhat horrifying nature of their facilities, Mumme made it clear to Wirth that he wanted his strength program to be run with the same intensity as a Division I program. Lower expectations in the preseason would naturally lead to lower expectations for the regular season, and both Mumme and Wirth agreed that was no way to get the results they were after. From day one, said Wirth, "We expected everything."

Wirth's lofty expectations for the effort of the players under his direction were matched and possibly exceeded by the effort that he put forth every day. Once Wirth arrived on Iowa Wesleyan's campus following his hour-long commute from Iowa City, he was a force of nature. The energy and enthusiasm that he brought to workouts were palpable throughout every session. Whether he was firing up the group for the day's lifts or firing tennis balls at receivers to work their hand–eye coordination, his effort set the tone for the entire team.

This is a great drill that we still do with our players today. We require that each of our receivers catch one hundred tennis balls per day. We taught our receivers and our running backs to catch footballs by catching tennis balls with their thumbs and forefingers. Today we use machines; but with no money for those kind of luxuries at Iowa Wesleyan, we proceeded to wear out the arms of our team managers.

Although Wirth's words and example made it clear that there were high expectations, he was also able to find common ground with Iowa Wesleyan's players when it came to designing workouts. Shortly into offseason workouts, Wirth identified offensive linemen John Coneset and Andrew Przybylski as the type of motivated leaders that could encourage and lead their peers as well as help him stay in tune with the pulse of the team. Periodically, the three of them would meet to break down the team's performance and get a feel for what workouts the team was responding to and what aspects of the training program they thought could be improved.

Wirth's discussions with his two-man leadership council proved to be a valuable tool for making adjustments to goals that would challenge the players and could realistically be achieved. Seven weeks into the team's first twelve-week weight training cycle, Wirth found that most of the players weren't making their lifts. The program he had the team on was a periodization cycle that increased the weight each player would lift each week on a variety of different exercises. After noticing the team's lack of progress and sitting down with Coneset and Przybylski to talk about how their bodies were responding to the program, Wirth realized that he was overtraining the players. Continued discussions provided him with the information he needed to implement training systems that would improve team strength by setting attainable goals. Those discussions would also set the precedent for the relationship Mumme's coaching staff would have with the football team at Iowa Wesleyan; it would be a partnership.

Mumme and his coaching staff were fully committed to winning games at Iowa Wesleyan, that much was evident in their tenacious recruiting efforts leading up to the season. That relentless drive to get better every day continued into offseason conditioning sessions with Wirth and would ultimately carry over into the team's first preseason practices together. Iowa Wesleyan's coaches hoped the players would take note of the example they were trying to set and ultimately share their work ethic and commitment to winning. But it's also true that beggars can't be choosers.

Six months is not an ideal timeframe for building a college football team's roster from scratch. Mumme and his fellow coaches recognized this, and although he had high expectations for the team that he would put on the field for Iowa Wesleyan, he recognized that simply fielding a team for the first game would be an accomplishment. Expecting an entire roster of new players to come into preseason on the same page with their coaches is unrealistic, particularly when the primary requirement to join the team was a just being a warm body. There was no way of knowing how many of them would respond to their new coaches and the unorthodox offensive scheme they planned to implement. Fortunately, Mumme and the rest of the coaching staff had a bridge to their freshly assembled and ever-evolving lineup in quarterback Dustin Dewald.

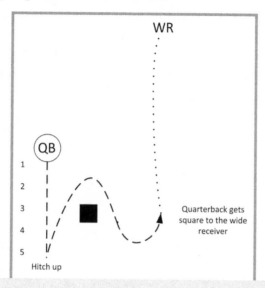

I look for a quarterback with great vision and great pocket feet. Dustin had both of these traits. We had our quarterbacks rep variations of this footwork drill during practice every week.

Dewald had exhibited a strong grasp of Mumme's pass-happy offense while he ran it at Copperas Cove, which was one of the main reasons Mumme pursued him as soon as he was named Iowa Wesleyan's new football coach. Furthermore, Dewald possessed the intangibles that commanded the respect of his teammates. Even going back to his high school days, Dewald owned the huddle. Mumme explained the dichotomy between Dewald's unassuming nature off the field and the persona he took on in the huddle this way: "To see him on the street you might wonder if he could check out a library book, but to hear him in the huddle sometimes you'd think he was leading them into battle." He came into camp with the quarterback job locked up in the minds of Iowa Wesleyan's coaching staff, but he was expected to compete just the same as the all the recruits who were joining the team with blank slates and earn his position.

Fortunately, it didn't take Dewald long to separate himself from the rest of the pack and emerge as the team's starting quarterback and undisputed leader. Physically, his arm strength wasn't exceptional, but as one wide receiver put it years after the fact, Dewald had the type of accuracy that "could take a dime out of my hands at 40 yards." That accuracy, combined with his understanding of the offense, made Dewald the ideal candidate to direct the Tigers aerial attack.

The other skill position players who ascended to the top of the depth chart provided Dewald with the tools he needed to make Iowa Wesleyan's offense one of the most prolific in the nation. Six months of aggressive recruiting by Mumme and Major loaded the Tigers' roster with talented players that had flown under the radar of NCAA football programs or been cast off from them for one reason or another.

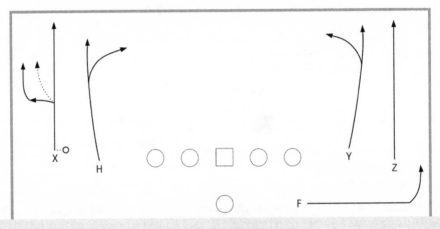

Our split end or "X" is usually our fastest receiver and that was where Chris Edwards played. He and Dustin had great chemistry from their days at Stephen F. Austin, and I tried to build on that familiarity when they came to Iowa Wesleyan. We gave Dustin and Chris freedom to make all the adjustments to the X-receiver's routes on their own. This is a diagram of our "6" call, the ultimate go-deep play and a basic Air Raid attack play.

The quick screen diagramed here (a play we also referred to as "19") was designed to get the ball to Chris Edwards early in the game and quickly became a staple of our offense, which it remains today.

Chris Edwards was a wide receiver who transferred to Iowa Wesleyan from Stephen F. Austin State University. Edwards' grades were fine, but he was ineligible to compete at the NCAA Division I level because the classes he had taken hadn't made enough progress toward the completion of a major. He and Dewald showed exceptional chemistry on the practice field during their lone season together in Nacogdoches, and head coach Jim Hess called Mumme to tell him as much when they discovered Dewald would be following his high school coach to Mount Pleasant. Fortunately for the Tigers, the NAIA didn't have any academic guidelines that would interfere with Edwards' eligibility.

The move from NCAA's Division I-AA to Division II of the NAIA represented a sharp decline in competition, and Iowa Wesleyan's coaching staff had high hopes for Edwards' performance come fall.

However, if he had gotten his way early on, he never would have stepped on the field for the Tigers. Edwards began attending classes at Iowa Wesleyan during the spring semester of 1989. Two weeks into classes he strolled up to Mumme's desk in the athletic office sporting a trench coat and a backpack filled with everything he needed to take his life back to his hometown of Livingston, Texas. Mumme, busy with administrative duties, looked up from his desk for a moment and asked Edwards what he could do for him. "Will you take me to the bus station?" Edwards asked his head coach.

"No," Mumme responded briskly before abruptly lowering his gaze back to the paperwork on his desk.

Exasperated, Edwards cried, "But I hate it here." Mumme could relate to the plight of his player. He shared Edwards' discomfort with their new, unpleasantly cold surroundings that were nearly one thousand miles from their respective homes. Mumme couldn't help but empathize with his player and took the time to again look up from his work and address Edwards' distress.

"Join the club, I hate it here too," he replied, before putting his head down and getting back to work. Half a minute of silence went by before Mumme was concerned enough to lift his head once more, and when he did, Edwards was gone. Edwards never did manage to get to the bus station that day, so he returned to his room to unpack and accepted the reality that he would be spending the next year of his life in Mount Pleasant.

Edwards' fellow pass-catchers, Marcus Washington and Dereck Hall, came from inner-city Chicago to Iowa Wesleyan by way of Triton Junior College in River Grove, Illinois. They were a package deal, with Hall easily being the more coveted of the two prospects. Washington hadn't caught a pass throughout his entire junior college career, and his academic transcripts were suspect, but having

31

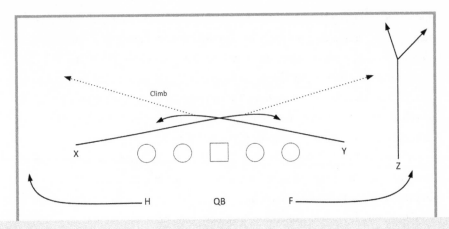

Marcus was our "Y" receiver and became great at sitting down on zone defenses and running climb routes against man coverage.

him on the team made Mount Pleasant a more desirable location for Hall, so Mumme decided to offer the two teammates spots on the roster.

Unfortunately for Mumme, the admissions department wasn't nearly as receptive to the idea of having Washington on campus as the coaching staff. When Mumme discovered that Washington's application had been rejected, he headed to the admissions office to demand an explanation as to why his recruit had been denied. A representative shared the admissions board's assessment of Washington's transcripts, which had led them to the conclusion that he simply was "not college material." Mumme disagreed and informed the board's messenger in no uncertain terms that he'd go directly over his head to the president if the admissions board wasn't willing to reconsider their assessment of Washington's college readiness. As was the case with a number of other contested admissions during Mumme's first recruiting season in Mount Pleasant, he found a way to get his players past a reluctant admissions office. However, the football program didn't wind up being the only beneficiary of Washington's admission to Iowa Wesleyan.

When Washington came to Iowa Wesleyan in August of 1989, something clicked for him that hadn't while he was attending school so close to home. In being so far away from home, Washington found a sense of responsibility in himself that had previously been dormant. He didn't want to go home without a degree, and he found that he preferred having cornfields and open space outside his window to crowded streets and tightly packed buildings as far as the eye could see. It wasn't long before Washington established himself as a leader within the football team, a role he was so comfortable in that he took on similar roles with the baseball and basketball teams at Iowa Wesleyan. Sports were going so well for Washington that he decided to start writing for the student newspaper as well. His involvement all over campus wound up getting him voted homecoming king his senior year. It was an impressive turnaround for someone who supposedly was not college material, to say the least.

The march to the admissions office became a dance that Mumme got familiar with throughout his first recruiting season. Iowa Wesleyan's admissions department was none too thrilled about all of the out-of-state applicants that the football program was funneling to the school, and they made a habit of rejecting the applications of Mumme's recruits. He may as well have had a standing weekly appointment with a member of the admissions board to air the program's grievances over the latest recruit who had been denied admission. For a school the size of Iowa Wesleyan it was a curious practice, but one that Mumme managed to remedy in most instances through reason, tenacity, and a sixth sense for finding the appropriate pressure point that would ultimately get him his way. However, not every questionable recruit that came to Mount Pleasant would go on to become a resounding success on par with Washington. As a matter of fact, there were some who became equally spectacular failures.

Another recruit whose application created a volatile battleground between Mumme and the admissions board was Iowa Wesleyan's prize defensive recruit who also came out of Triton Junior College. Mike Jefferson was a six-foot, seven-inch, 310-pound nose tackle from Chicago whose physical stature was matched only by his considerable baggage, which was probably the only thing that stood between him and playing big-time college football. Triton's head coach took the time to explain Jefferson's issues to Mumme during a meeting between the three of them early in the recruiting process. Triton's coach spoke about his nose tackle's size, abilities, and on-field resume, which should have landed him on a Big 10 roster had it not been for a rather substantial catch. "One thing you need to know is that Mike loves to fight," explained his coach before looking to his nose tackle for an affirmation, "Don't you, Mike?" Jefferson, slumped over in his chair so badly that Mumme nearly forgot he was six-foot-seven, nodded his head as he kept his eyes fixated on the floor. "But," he went on, "he never wins. Do you, Mike?" to which Jefferson shook his head, maintaining his steadfast gaze on the ground. Desperate for a playmaker on the defensive side of the ball,

Mumme chose to ignore his better judgment and offered Jefferson a spot on Iowa Wesleyan's roster. It wouldn't take long to regret that decision.

When Mumme's first training camp at Iowa Wesleyan began, his and the rest of the coaching staff's most difficult task was getting sixty different personalities and agendas from all over the country onto the same page. Fortunately, the coaching staff had a number of forces working in their favor heading into camp. For one thing, it helped that the team was composed of players who had chosen to come to play football at Iowa Wesleyan. In most cases, it was an indication they were serious about the game. They simply wouldn't have chosen to go there otherwise. Mount Pleasant was an hour drive from anything that resembled a city and no one had ever mistaken the social scene on campus for "vibrant." Free of distractions, the players who came to camp had few options other than to put in the work required to prepare for the season.

The overhauled roster also gave Iowa Wesleyan's football team the fresh start it so desperately needed. Coming off of a 0–10 season and a four-year stretch of 9–31, the best memory of the program's recent past was no memory. New players allowed the team to focus on the future and believe in what they were capable of achieving without reservation.

Finally, although he was new to Mount Pleasant, Iowa Wesleyan's starting quarterback Dewald had plenty of experience with Mumme's offense and a year of college football under his belt. Although he came into camp with the starting job pretty much locked up, he quickly emerged as a team leader because of his skill set and maturity. However, that didn't necessarily sit well with everyone on the roster. Mumme had also recruited a quarterback out of a nearby junior college named Jay Eardly, just as a contingency in the event that Dewald got injured.

Naturally, Eardly's agenda differed from Mumme's in that he came to campus expecting to be the starter. Within the first few practices it became clear that Dewald had a superior grasp of the offense. Several practices later, Eardly's position on the depth chart became clear when he started watching Dewald take all of the first-team reps at quarterback. After a couple of days on the sideline he stormed into Mumme's office and demanded to know why he hadn't been told that Mumme brought his high school quarterback to campus. Mumme looked back at him for a moment and calmly replied, "You never asked." The next day Eardly's locker was empty and Mumme was left with Dewald as his only plausible option at quarterback.

Not wanting to see the Tigers' season go up in flames if Dewald were to get hurt, Mumme got to work re-recruiting the best option on campus, fifth-year senior Tim

Smith. Also a talented catcher who had tryouts with a couple of major league teams, Smith had led Iowa Wesleyan's single wing attack the previous season. When he was initially presented the idea, Smith wasn't interested in putting on the pads again unless he could be the starter. Mumme refused to take no for an answer and was ultimately able to cajole Smith into rejoining the team when he explained that the team had no other viable options at quarterback and agreed not to bring Smith in for mop-up duty at the end of blowouts. If Dewald went down, Smith would become the starter. Otherwise, Smith would be free to take soft toss on the sidelines or work on tightening up his throw to second base for all Mumme cared. The situation certainly wasn't ideal, but it was an arrangement everyone could live with.

Tim Smith has gone on to have an outstanding high school coaching career as a quarterback coach at a number of Texas high schools. After graduating from Iowa Wesleyan and pursuing a career in professional baseball, he took my advice and moved to the Lone Star State to coach high school football.

By late August, Iowa Wesleyan's revamped football team was gradually coming into its own. The talented recruits the coaching staff brought to Mount Pleasant figured to physically outmatch the majority of their opponents and the offense seemed to be finding a rhythm around Dewald. When the team shellacked William Penn in a scrimmage one Saturday afternoon, Mumme rewarded his team's performance with a day off on Sunday. He proceeded to head home feeling great about the team he had assembled and their effort that day. That feeling was shattered around 2 A.M. when Mumme received a phone call from a police officer requesting his presence in town because Mike Jefferson's arm was stuck in the side of a house.

As it turned out, a number of the players headed to a party that night to celebrate their victory and to take advantage of their day off. The evening went on without incident until the early morning hours when a confrontation involving Jefferson arose. Words were exchanged between Jefferson and another partygoer, tensions rose, and tempers flared to the point that he got riled up enough to drive his fist through the side of the house next door. Jefferson's forearm wound up getting stuck in the siding and he couldn't remove his arm for fear of mangling it further with the sharp splintered wood surrounding the hole he had just created.

When Mumme arrived to find his best defensive player's right arm held captive by splinters from the home's siding, Jefferson explained, "I just got so upset and I didn't wanna hit anybody so I hit the house." Understandably, the owner of the house was unmoved by Jefferson's apparent show of restraint and called the police, who called Mumme, who assured the owner of the house that Jefferson would cover the cost of the damages he inflicted on his home. Only then did the homeowner agree to help free Jefferson's arm from the side of his house, which ironically delivered him deep into Mumme's doghouse.

4

THE FIRST SEASON

In a town full of people with deep roots in the community, Bob Lamm was no exception. He was born in Mount Pleasant to parents who had also been born and raised in Henry County. After serving in the Navy during World War II, Lamm's father set up a barber shop in town. It wasn't long after that his wife had a son and the younger Lamm was out making his own fun with his friends in town. In Mount Pleasant, that meant playing sports. Lamm spent his summer days in the small town playing Little League baseball at McLellan Park or organizing sandlot games with the other available children in the neighborhood. Even if there were only seven kids there, they would figure out a way to play football, basketball, baseball, or whatever game that they could agree on. The few days that didn't consist of sports sun up to sun down were spent at the local swimming pool, presumably with the likes of Scotty Smalls, Benny "The Jet" Rodriquez, Michael "Squints" Palledorous, and the rest of the cast of *The Sandlot* scheming on the lifeguard, Wendy Peffercorn.

In 1962, Lamm graduated from Mount Pleasant High School along with most of his childhood playmates, and like many of his fellow graduates, he chose to put down roots in his hometown. The town didn't have many big attractions to offer outside of the Midwest Old Thresher's Reunion that Mount Pleasant hosted each Labor Day weekend, but every day provided little things, fun things, hokey things, and smiling familiar faces to keep life simple and enjoyable. Lamm also managed to mix things up enough to keep life interesting throughout the time he

37

spent in his hometown. He served seven years in the Iowa National Guard, owned a restaurant for a while, worked in sales, spent some time on the air as a DJ for the local radio station, officiated high school football and basketball games, ran a car wash, and got married a couple times.

Throughout all that time and all those jobs, Lamm's involvement with the Iowa Wesleyan Booster Club remained a constant. Another constant was the football team's reliably dismal performance each fall. With the exception of a couple winning seasons under Tom Horne in the early 1980s, the team was uninspiring and most locals paid little attention to the product Iowa Wesleyan was putting onto the gridiron. Lamm was an exception, and he wanted to do all he could to make sure Mumme succeeded when he was hired to coach the Tigers. That desire led Lamm into the athletic office to lend his insight on how to garner the community's financial support when Mumme arrived in February, and it also led him to Iowa Wesleyan's sideline when the Tigers kicked off a new era of football at Mapleleaf Field in Mount Pleasant on September 23, 1989.

The 1989 season looked to be a special one for Tiger faithfuls like Lamm. Mumme's hiring appeared to be a signal that Iowa Wesleyan's administration was finally committing itself to fielding a competitive football team. For the first time in years, the school affiliated its football team with a league, the Illini-Badger-Hawkeye Football Conference. What's more, Mumme and Mike Major had brought a number of talented players to Mount Pleasant in their seven months on the job, and the support of the school and loyal members of the booster club had helped to make that possible. The team's more optimistic fans figured the team had a shot at actually winning a few games.

Unfortunately, the two road games leading up to Iowa Wesleyan's home opener hadn't exactly gone according to plan. Two weeks previously the Tigers began their season in a road contest against University of Dubuque. The offense never quite found its rhythm as Dustin Dewald and company only managed to put up 264 yards through the air, a modest output considering what the group proved themselves to be capable of later in the season. The result was a 22–19 loss, but not everybody was disappointed with the outcome, particularly college president Dr. Robert Prins.

After the game, Prins made a point to seek out his head coach, pat him on the back, and let him know how impressed he was with the football program's progress in Mumme's short time on campus. Iowa Wesleyan's football team was actually competitive, and the program was generating so much interest around the community that the booster club managed to fill a charter bus with fans for the three hundred-mile round trip to Dubuque to watch the season opener. People were enthusiastic about Iowa Wesleyan football and that was enough for Prins. Not surprisingly, the sentiment wasn't shared in the Tigers' locker room.

A week later, the team made the trip to Canton, Missouri, to face off against Culver-Stockton College. While the offense was on the field, Leach began something of a tradition, in which he would prowl the sidelines and occasionally get into Mumme's ear to make sure his head coach was keeping an aggressive mind-set. "Don't stop attacking," Leach would say as he crept up behind Mumme before backing off to give his head coach room to think. As simple an idea as it was, it would go on to become something of a guiding principle for their offensive approach, and an effective one at that. It paid dividends because Dewald and company improved their production, but the Tigers lost another heartbreaker, 31–28.

Although the season began with two losses, leading up to Iowa Wesleyan's home opener versus Grinnell College, there was a prevailing sense of optimism among the team as well as its fans. For fans like Lamm, it probably had something to do with the stark improvement in the team's competitiveness. The Tigers wound up on the wrong end of 52–0, 40–0, 39–0, and 41–2 outcomes over the course of the previous season's 0–10 effort, and a competent offense gave fans something to cheer for. Iowa Wesleyan's players found reason for hope in the knowledge that just about everyone was new to the program, and they were only a couple of breaks away from coming into the game undefeated. And coaches found reassurance in the game film that Grinnell College sent them earlier in the week; the sideline angle of which repeatedly panned from the playing field to an area beyond one of the end zones where something of a scantily-clad volleyball game was in progress. The film was a masterpiece of ham-fisted football and soft-core pornography that left Mumme and his staff salivating for Iowa Wesleyan's first gridiron victory in nearly two years. "I knew right then we were gonna kick their ass," recalled Mumme of watching Grinnell's distracted reel of game film.

The Tigers quickly proved Mumme to be a visionary when they raced to a 26–7 halftime lead on touchdown passes from Dewald to Chris Edwards, Marcus Washington, and Dereck Hall. The Tigers kept their foot firmly on the accelerator in the second half as Dewald found teammates Mike Black, Lafayette Prince, and Edwards again for touchdowns. When the game came to a close, Iowa Wesleyan emerged with a 49–7 victory and Dewald's six touchdown passes set a new single-game record for the Tigers, the first of dozens he would establish over the course of his three-year career at Iowa Wesleyan.

The following week, the Tigers rode the momentum from the Grinnell College thrashing to Sheboygan, Wisconsin, where they beat Lakeland College, 21–7. This was the team's first league contest, and Lakeland came into the game as the favorite to take home the conference title. Beating Lakeland brought an air of legitimacy to the program that the Grinnell victory had not. Furthermore, it provided a much-needed confidence boost to a team that was still getting familiar with one another and learning what they could accomplish together.

A week later in Jacksonville, Illinois, the team learned a little more when they beat MacMurray College, 38–0, and set twelve school records in the process. The team established new school standards for passing attempts, completions, passing yards, and total yards in addition to establishing new defensive highs in sacks and punts by an opponent. In addition, Major's defense didn't just pitch a shutout; they didn't even allow MacMurray's offense to gain a first down.

A week later, a showdown with Greenville College waited. The Tigers' resentment for Greenville had no shortage of layers. First and foremost, the two schools were tied for first place in the conference and the winner of the game would have an inside track to the conference championship and the automatic berth in the NAIA playoffs that came with it. Then there was the issue of residual bad blood from the vicious beating the Panthers bestowed on the Tigers a year earlier, to the tune of 52–0. Granted, Iowa Wesleyan's roster was composed almost exclusively of players who weren't even aware the two schools existed before their recruitment, but the significance of a victory over Greenville given their recent history resonated in the Tigers' locker room just the same.

On a more personal level, Mumme wanted this game in the worst way possible. When his players lined up on the field against Greenville, he would be lined up on the sidelines across from his former colleague and rival, Max Bowman. The two worked together on Bill Yung's staff at University of Texas El Paso. Mumme orchestrated the passing attack whereas Bowman coordinated the ground game, and each coach believed their domain boasted the superior offensive approach. It created a fair amount of tension between the two that never materialized in any sort of real conflict. However, their divergent methods for moving the football did manifest themselves in two strikingly different, yet similarly successful, offenses when the former colleagues finally had the opportunity to create football teams in the image of their respective offensive visions. Bowman's Panthers rolled into

Mount Pleasant with the nation's most prolific rushing offense whereas the Tigers boasted the nation's fourth-best passing game. Conflicting offensive philosophies and two sound football teams were on a collision course for Mapleleaf Field.

Lamm and the rest of the Iowa Wesleyan Booster Club chose to gear up for the occasion by hosting a chili cook-off in the parking lot before the game. The community came out in droves to sample the chili and authentic Texas barbecue being served by the parents of Iowa Wesleyan's players who had come into town for the game. However, because of the previous year's lopsided outcome, few of the fans chose to stick around beyond the pregame culinary festivities. When kickoff finally arrived, the stands at Mapleleaf field were fairly empty. Those that stayed were treated to a first half that showed how far the Tigers had come under Mumme's direction.

Iowa Wesleyan began the afternoon's scoring when Edwards grabbed a 44-yard touchdown pass from than Dewald early in the first quarter, and the rest of the game played out like an afternoon with the Cowboys and Earp brothers at the OK Corral. The two combatants took a break from the shootout at halftime with the Tigers holding a 20–17 edge over the Panthers. When the two teams took the field for the second half, they resumed hostilities in front of a crowd that had grown significantly. Although most of the fans hadn't been willing to buy tickets at the start of the game, a number of people throughout town tuned in for the radio broadcast and had a change of heart. When Iowa Wesleyan managed to not only be competitive in the first half, but actually also take a lead into halftime, a number of fans chose to return to Mapleleaf Field to cheer on the Tigers.

There was no shortage of excitement in the second half. Dewald connected with Hall and Washington for touchdowns as running backs Derick Callis and Derrick Wagoner scampered for touchdowns of 47 and 6 yards, respectively. Kicker Duncan Brown added a field goal to bring the Tigers' offensive output on the afternoon to 46. Dewald threw for 432 yards in the game and Callis and Wagoner added 106 more on the ground. However, it wasn't enough to overcome the 47 points that Greenville put up on 563 yards of total offense, and Iowa Wesleyan lost by a single point.

Despite the loss, the competitive showcase the contrasting styles delivered that day earned the attention of a number of members of the Mount Pleasant community who had been slow to come around on Iowa Wesleyan football. The game's close outcome brought credibility and some much deserved recognition to what was taking place at Iowa Wesleyan. "It kind of made our program even though we didn't win it," said Mumme as he reflected on the game and its aftermath.

The program was generating interest around the community and Mumme's pass-happy offense was capturing the imaginations of football fans throughout the Hawkeye State. Lamm and the rest of the Mount Pleasant community watched as people from all over descended on their town on Saturday afternoons in the autumn of 1989 to see an offensive revolution taking its baby steps. Each Saturday the Iowa Wesleyan Tigers were preaching the gospel of the spread offense, and pilgrims from across Iowa and the Midwest were flocking to Mount Pleasant to catch a glimpse of it. The Tigers did not disappoint.

The team followed the offensive spectacle versus Greenville by dismantling University of Chicago 34–9 in business-like fashion. Along the way, Dewald set the school record for most passing yards in a single season with three games remaining on the schedule.

A week later, Edwards and Washington combined to reel in fifteen passes for more than 300 yards in a 54–23 beating of Central Methodist University that featured a bench-clearing brawl in the end zone after Iowa Wesleyan's final touchdown of the afternoon. The altercation certainly had something to do with the prevailing sentiment on the Eagles' sideline that the Tigers were running up the score, but it also may have had something to do with the fact that it had been a strikingly bizarre afternoon.

Halloween was right around the corner, but most agree that the source of at least some of the strange vibes floating around Mapleleaf Field that crisp October day was one of the usual suspects, Lamm. According to most eyewitness accounts of the afternoon's events, Lamm spent the first half of the game making the most of his sideline privileges by verbally lambasting the officials from point-blank range. Seemingly every call provided more fuel for his relentless vitriol for the referees, who Lamm seemed to be convinced, had it out for Iowa Wesleyan that day.

Naturally, Lamm shares a different version of the story. He claims that he was merely making some critical comments about a single call to an Iowa Wesleyan player on the sideline that an official with rabbit ears happened to overhear.

Whether it was the result of unyielding verbal abuse or oversensitivity, all interested parties agree that one of the referees approached Mumme as he walked to the locker room at halftime and thrust an angry index finger in Lamm's direction. "Do you know that guy over there?" he demanded. Mumme took a patronizing glance in Lamm's direction to sell the words that came out of his mouth next.

"I've never seen him before in my life." With that, the referee proceeded to banish Lamm to the far corner of the bleachers, as far away from the action as possible, for the remainder of the game.

When the second half got underway, nose tackle Mike Jefferson took up Lamm's mantle for unbecoming behavior and went into what had become his standard routine of taking cheap shots at opponents after the whistle. Over the course of the season, Jefferson had gotten into the habit of committing the type of egregious personal fouls from Hollywood movies that galvanize the good guys to mount a furious and improbable comeback. During the Central Methodist game the belligerent practice reached its fever pitch, and shortly into the third quarter he shoved a Central Methodist player to the ground well after the play had ended as he made his way back to the huddle. Somehow, the officials missed the shove and failed to throw a flag, but it did draw the ire of Mumme who was coming to the conclusion that Jefferson's considerable ability wasn't worth the interminable string of headaches he provided.

"MIKE!" Mumme shouted from the sidelines before making eye contact with his nose tackle and making it clear that one more act of aggression would put an end to his time playing football at Iowa Wesleyan. Jefferson's obedience lasted all of two plays before he drew a fifteen-yard personal foul for shoving another Central Methodist player after the whistle. Mumme called Jefferson off the field immediately and informed him that he had just played his final down for Iowa Wesleyan. Then things really got weird.

Infuriated, Jefferson began marching to the locker room sporting his full uniform and equipment, but it didn't end that way. As he stomped off the field, Jefferson removed equipment and articles of clothing as he went. He began the striptease by ripping off his helmet and throwing it to the fence, which was promptly followed by his jersey and shoulder pads. It's unclear what came after that, but by the time a student manager drew Mumme's attention to the walking metaphor taking his final steps into the locker room, Jefferson was donning little more than a girdle. The trail of gear in Jefferson's wake was hastily gathered by the student assistant as the attention of everyone on hand returned to the lopsided game in progress.

On Monday morning, Jefferson returned to the athletic offices to offer a tearful apology for the charade and to beg for his spot on the team back. Mumme would not have any of it. "You've embarrassed us too much," he told his former player. Besides, it wasn't fair to his teammates to have to deal with the distraction or the penalties that resulted from his increasingly erratic behavior on the field.

With Jefferson off the team and Lamm living in fear of exile, the proceedings with Blackburn College the following week were substantially more civil, but the outcome was similar as the Tigers coasted to a 47–10 victory, a 5–1 conference record, and a second place finish in the Illini-Badger-Hawkeye conference. However, the game was not without its own compelling subplot. Before the game, Leach's wife Sharon went into labor with the couple's second child. The Leach family raced to the hospital, but once they got there Mike was determined to do all that he could to contribute to Iowa Wesleyan's efforts. As Sharon was in labor, Mike bounced back and forth between the delivery room and a phone in the waiting room to call receivers coach David Johnsen in the press box. Leach would get a play-by-play and then would proceed to offer feedback and suggestions based on the descriptions of the game that Johnsen was giving him. Although the game wasn't competitive, Leach was unwavering in his commitment to the team.

With the Tigers holding a commanding 27–10 lead halfway through the third quarter, Johnsen suggested that Leach get back to his wife. After some discussion, Leach finally acquiesced and returned to the delivery room for good to welcome his and Sharon's second daughter, Kim, into the world. For good measure, Dewald tossed three more touchdown passes in the fourth quarter.

The following week, a twist with Trinity College brought a close to the regular season with a 28–18 win. At season's end, the Tigers boasted a 7–3 record, and they did it running one of the most exciting collegiate offenses in the country, regardless of the school's size or competitive affiliation. Dewald's performance at quarterback put him among the NAIA's national leaders in most passing categories. Naturally, the people of southeast Iowa wanted to see more, and the Tigers were more than happy to oblige.

A couple days after the shootout with Greenville back in October, the Tigers' innovative offense had created a buzz in the area around Mount Pleasant, even among those who weren't Iowa Wesleyan insiders. Nearby Burlington was just such a community. It was a small town in its own right, but its population of twenty-seven thousand was more than three times the size of Mount Pleasant and hence a popular destination for area singles that enjoyed dabbling in the little nightlife that southeast Iowa had to offer.

Among those singles was Iowa Wesleyan's defensive coordinator, Mike Major. During the time he spent out and about in Burlington, Major struck up a friendship with Lance Gardner, a local businessman and leader in the community. One night shortly after the Greenville game, the two were sitting at a bar when Gardner made a comment to the effect of, "I wish you guys could come to Burlington and play a game so we could watch you play." The passing comment got Major thinking, "What if we could?"

The next day, Major presented the possibility of staging a postseason game in Burlington to Mumme. He was intrigued by the idea. For years, LaVell Edwards' high flying BYU teams were shut out of major bowl games because their Mormon fan base didn't drink, eliminating some of the boost the local economy would receive from hosting the game. All of that changed when San Diego's Mormon community organized the Holiday Bowl, a game that featured BYU the first eight years of its existence. If Iowa Wesleyan couldn't get invited to the postseason, they would just stage their own game. It certainly seemed like a reasonable option, and Mumme kept the idea in the back of his mind while he kept his focus on winning the remaining games on the schedule to earn a berth in the NAIA playoffs. As the season wore on and it became apparent that Greenville would be taking home the league title and going to the playoffs, Mumme and the rest of the coaching staff began exploring the possibility of hosting a postseason game more seriously.

The effort began by poring through the NAIA rulebook to see what sort of guidelines it put forth regarding postseason play outside of the national playoffs. The rulebook provided a process to go through to host a sanctioned bowl game. Because the coaching staff was looking into the matter so late into the season there was no way they would be able to meet all the requirements to host an NAIA-sanctioned bowl game. However, the rule book didn't prevent teams from competing in nonsanctioned games after the season's completion. Naturally, Mumme saw the NAIA's omission as an opportunity.

With two weeks left in the season, Mumme put the chain of events that would lead to the Steamboat Classic into action. Some members of the coaching staff as well as Mumme's wife began visiting businesses around town in search of sponsors for the game, and others started placing phone calls to schools around the country in search of an opponent that would be willing to pay their way to southeast Iowa to play a football game in the middle of December.

When all the phone calls and solicitations had been made, Lambuth College's 8–2 football team that finished the season ranked 25 in the country agreed to make the 470-mile journey from Jackson, Tennessee, to Burlington. A variety of local businesses put up advertising dollars that covered the cost of programs and the facilities charges of Burlington High School's Bracewell Stadium. The Burlington chapter of the United Way became the recipient of the game's gate receipts.

Regardless of the game's outcome, its mere existence constituted a monumental success for the program. When the season began, Iowa Wesleyan's administration was hesitant to charge admission to the team's home games at Mapleleaf Field; they were concerned that no one cared enough about the team to actually pay to see them play. The fact that people were spending their time, money, and energy to stage one more game for the team spoke volumes about how far the program had come in less than a year's time. Considering the effort and support that the community put forth to make the Steamboat Classic a reality, the outcome of the game almost didn't matter when it came to taking inventory of wins and losses. The day itself was a victory for the program, win or lose.

The inaugural United Way Steamboat Football Classic saw people in and around the Mount Pleasant community leap at the opportunity to see Iowa Wesleyan's high flying offense one last time, and they weren't disappointed. The Tigers and the Eagles combined for 96 points on 1,112 yards of total offense. Although the Tigers lost the game 55–41, fans got to see Dewald sling the ball around the field one last time before another long, cold Iowa winter set in. However, there was one big difference between the winter that lay ahead and winters past: Lamm and the rest of Iowa Wesleyan's football fans actually believed they had something to look forward to next fall.

5

ENTER CHARLIE MOOT

The traditions, rituals, and pageantry of college football are a bit misleading in the sense that they disguise a universal truth familiar to any head coach who's managed to maintain some level of success for a period of time: things change. Whether it's an expected change like players graduating and a new crop of recruits coming to campus or an unforeseen change like the sudden departure of a valued member of the coaching staff for another job, there is little that remains constant. Regardless of the change's origins, be it necessity, observation, curiosity, or some other derivation, good coaches and the successful programs they oversee are in a constant state of evolution. Despite the fact that a good portion of the roster would be returning to the Tigers in 1990, the offseason following Iowa Wesleyan's 1989 campaign was a shining example of this principle.

Few members of the Iowa Wesleyan community, if any, enjoyed the Steamboat Classic as much as college president Robert Prins. The game afforded him the opportunity to climb the steps at Bracewell Stadium through a sea of enthusiastic fans to find his spot in the press box and watch those same fans cheer on the home team in a game that they helped to create. The Steamboat Classic was a proud day for Prins, especially considering the fact that the Tiger's participation in such an event seemed unfathomable only a few months beforehand. The game made it apparent that Tiger football and Iowa Wesleyan mattered within the community. Anxious to do what he could to ensure that those displays of school spirit continued, Prins called Mumme

47

into his office the following week to ask a simple question: "What can I do to help you?"

It was a question that Mumme had been considering quite a bit after the season's end. He wanted to do right by Mike Major, whose loyalty in following Mumme from Copperas Cove to Mount Pleasant had also resulted in a colossal pay cut. Retaining Mike Leach, whose talent for coaching had already become apparent, was also a priority for Mumme. "Mike Leach and Mike Major," Mumme began, "we need to double their salaries." It didn't take long to get Prins to agree to those terms.

The pay grade for Leach and Major was so low during the 1989 season that doubling their salaries had only raised their socioeconomic status from destitute to impoverished, but it was an improvement nonetheless. Despite the still meager compensation, the extra scratch allowed the Leach family's lifestyle to make a crucial leap.

Leach and his wife Sharon spent their first year in Mount Pleasant in a trailer that Iowa Wesleyan allowed them to live in rent free, a financial necessity given Leach's meager salary during his first year. The tiny dwelling found itself in the midst of a jungle of other mobile homes and unkempt foliage where a variety of discarded appliances and other larger refuse often lurked. The trailer park safari continued through the front door of the Leach family mobile home and onto the floor, ceiling, and walls that were tastefully ornamented with aggressive red shag carpeting as far as the eye could see. Additional excitement in the home was provided by the ceiling fan that hung at neck level and perpetually rotated at treacherous speeds usually reserved for the propellers of commercial jets.

The raise allowed Leach and his growing family to afford more aesthetically pleasing and less perilous accommodations, which would lead the growing family to a quaint house behind an insurance office in town. Sharon was pleased. Mike was happy too, but he wanted to take advantage of his new home's inviting and well-manicured lawn to bring some southern California panache to the Midwest. Ultimately, he settled on planting corn stalks alongside the walkway to his new front door, and the palm trees of a Los Angeles boulevard collided with Grant Wood's *American Gothic*. After nearly a year of living in Mount Pleasant, the Leach family was finally home.

Major proved to be far less interested in settling down in Mount Pleasant. Without a family or any other obligations beyond his employment to bound him to his current location, Major was free to follow any new opportunities that might come along. Thanks to his tenacious recruiting efforts the previous offseason and the team's performance in the fall, it seemed inevitable that a new opportunity would present itself soon.

When Iowa Wesleyan managed to lure Dustin Dewald and wide receiver Chris Edwards to southeast Iowa from Stephen F. Austin State University, the Lumberjacks' head coach Lynn Graves took notice. That led to a conversation between Graves and Major at January's American Football Coaches Association Convention in San Francisco, during which Graves learned more about the job Major had done recruiting central Texas as well as the rest of the country leading up to the 1989 season. Graves figured he could use a tireless recruiter like that on his coaching staff, and he decided to offer Major a job with Stephen F. Austin as the team's recruiting coordinator.

Taking the job at Stephen F. Austin would be a big step forward for Major's coaching career, there was no way that he could turn it down. Even so, it was difficult for him to leave behind a program he helped to build that was full of kids that he recruited. Leaving Mumme, a coach whose fortunes had risen and fallen with his own for more than a decade, wouldn't be any easier. So with a hopeful and heavy heart, Major strode into Mumme's hotel room to deliver the news that he would be accepting the job at Stephen F. Austin. He explained to his head coach that the job at Stephen F. Austin would be a great move for his career, that the salary would be a massive increase, and listed a number of additional perks that would come along with the new job. A seemingly unmoved Mumme could only shake his head and sneer, "That's great, but if you had any loyalty at all you would turn it down."

A few moments of uncomfortable silence ensued as Major stared back at Mumme with a look of consternation while the latter did his best to keep a straight face and continue to sell the ruse. Before long Mumme's face broke into a smile and the two colleagues shared a laugh and congratulations. Mumme was happy to see his friend move on to a higher profile job and return to Division I football. This also left Mumme behind with the difficult task of replacing his long-time defensive coordinator. It wouldn't be the only job that he would have to fill during the offseason.

The first addition to the staff was defensive backs coach Rickey Watts, a former wide receiver for the Chicago Bears. Watts came to Iowa Wesleyan from Cameron University in Oklahoma and brought a talented wide receiver by the name of Bruce Carter with him. Iowa Wesleyan's new wide receivers coach Lonnie Powers came to Iowa Wesleyan from Lone Tree High School in Iowa where he had been the head football coach. Mike Fanoga, a former player for Mumme at the University of Texas at El Paso, came to the Tiger's coaching staff from the University of West Alabama where he coached linebackers.

The final addition to Iowa Wesleyan's coaching staff was Charlie Moot, who Mumme had also worked with at the University of Texas at El Paso. Mumme initially brought him on as an assistant coach, but after Major took the job at Stephen F. Austin, Moot became the best candidate on staff to replace the departed defensive coordinator. Moot had never coordinated a defense before, but Mumme knew that he could count on Moot to be loyal and outwork anyone else that he might have considered for the job. Experience would come, and Moot seemed to be ready to take on the new role and the increased responsibility that came with it.

Iowa Wesleyan's new defensive coordinator was a short, stocky, bald man of the Danny DeVito mold whose most egregious offense against humanity was a nearly criminal deficiency of self-awareness. It also may have been his defining character trait. However, those who came to know him best found it difficult to hold Moot's dearth of social grace against him; it was entirely possible that his brain had stockpiled survival instincts to the point that there just wasn't room left for anything else. "Charlie was loveably oblivious to the world around him," Mumme laughed more than twenty years later.

"Charlie was a world-class scavenger," reflected Leach as he offered up choice stories from his mental rolodex of shortcuts Moot would employ to navigate the sea of financial turmoil that accompanied the life of a small-time college assistant coach. For instance, it was hardly a rare occurrence to see Moot making his way around town with a trunk full of empty bottles and cans in pursuit of more of the same. He would regularly pay visits to friends and local businesses to ask if he could rummage through their refuse in search of recyclables that he could haul off to a nearby recycling center to redeem for a few cents apiece.

Then there was Moot's illicit use of the gas card issued to him by Iowa Wesleyan. One of his favorite pastimes was going to the gas station to pick up a twelve-pack of Milwaukee's Best and requesting that the attendant mark his purchase as antifreeze. "He would buy antifreeze every day," remembered Leach.

Those same survival instincts, combined with his tenacity in practice and on the sidelines come game day, proved to be what would make Moot a good fit as Iowa Wesleyan's defensive coordinator. As remains the case today, running a defense under Mumme is not for the faint of heart. There are seemingly few things he hates more than seeing his defense on the field. Offensively, if Mumme wasn't going for it on 4th and 6 from his own 38-yard line, he was calling in a fake punt on 4th and 17 from his own 23-yard line. On the occasions that the offense or the punt team wasn't successful in converting a first down, Moot's defense found itself defending a short field. When such situations arose, Moot was the type of guy would briefly curse his luck and his head coach before getting down to coaching up his defense to keep the opposition off the scoreboard.

Except when he was told not to keep the opposition off the scoreboard, which occurred more often than most would expect. It wasn't uncommon for players and coaches to find Mumme prowling the sidelines and yelling at Moot, "Charlie, if you can't stop 'em, let 'em score." It wasn't quite the vote of confidence a defensive coordinator hopes to receive from his head coach. However, Moot was able to see what his head coach was really trying to get across, which was that it was alright to take some chances defensively because the Tigers had an offense that would forgive those types of aggressive mistakes on the scoreboard.

Whatever the situation, Moot was a passionate coach who brought a unique energy to the defensive side of the ball and his fire for the game was regularly communicated to his players in amusing fashion. "You need to stop being a bunch of Tom Turkeys and play some football," Moot would shout at his defense from the sideline. The terminology he used during practice was equally unconventional. If one of his players was having a difficult time making tackles or looked off balance he was fond of telling them, "You need to go out and get yourself some new traction masters." The nomenclature Moot employed around the team quickly became a favorite topic of discussion among players and coaches.

Moot's residency in Mount Pleasant began in the Mumme family home on a twin bed in the room of the Mumme's fifteen-year-old son Matt. June signed off on the arrangement under the presumption that Moot would be actively searching for a less invasive living arrangement and that his time in the Mumme household was only a temporary arrangement. Moot's understanding of the situation differed in a few key respects.

Being single and a bit of a domestic rube, Moot had little experience to draw from to empathize with June's reluctance to raise her children with someone who was essentially a stranger running around the house. Conversely, Moot believed that if he regularly did the dishes after mealtime and kept the refrigerator stocked with a quart of his world-class salsa he was doing his part to earn his keep in the Mumme household. June had other ideas, and so did the Mummes' six-year-old

51

daughter Leslie who had begun astutely, if not discourteously, referring to the family's houseguest as "Coach Mooch."

Nine days into Moot's tenure in Mount Pleasant, Mumme walked into the kitchen to find his wife trembling over the sink. When he asked what was wrong, June turned around, her face on the verge of tears. She confessed that Moot's constant presence was driving her and the kids crazy, that Leslie had taken to calling him Coach Mooch, and filed a variety of other grievances against their houseguest. It was clear that Moot's stay had to come to a close. She ended the conversation by asking, "Do you want to tell him or me?" With that, after nearly a week and a half in the Mumme household, Coach Mooch was sent packing to find a living arrangement more befitting a forty-five-year-old man.

Clearly, Moot was not a man for all occasions, particularly those on the domestic front. But for his recruiting partner Leach, more often than not, Moot proved to make for a fine companion. For someone with a mind as curious as Leach's, someone as uninhibited as Moot may have been the perfect muse.

As another grey and icy Iowa winter dug in its heels in southeast Iowa, Mumme gave Leach and Moot orders to head south on a recruiting trip through Missouri, Arkansas, Texas, Mississippi, Alabama, and Florida. They made the trip together in Moot's Dodge Dynasty counting the hours, miles, and recruits that passed as they made their way through the southland all the way to the Sunshine State. With so much time for the two of them to pass together, the conversation frequently drifted to things besides football and the day's recruiting visits. Occasionally, Moot would even wax nostalgic about his days pledging a fraternity as an undergraduate at Ithaca College in upstate New York. During one such instance, Moot began by complaining, "People today just aren't tough." Unsure of exactly what his companion was getting at, Leach requested that Moot elaborate on that assertion.

"What's tough?" he asked with his customary deadpan delivery. It could've been any number of things, really. Moot had been a Marine during the Vietnam War, and several minutiae of the late 1980s and early 1990s cultural zeitgeist couldn't have been sitting well with him: Nintendo, mullets, or New Kids on the Block to name a few. Whatever it was, the fads of the day just didn't look quite enough like his own rough-and-tumble adolescence to earn Moot's stamp of approval.

"You know what's tough?" Moot asked rhetorically as he drove along and further considered his point. "Back at Ithaca, me and one of my fraternity brothers would have to sit naked in a tub together. We'd have to pound a beer, then eat a raw egg, pound a beer then eat a raw egg until we puked all over each other. Now that was tough." A man of lesser curiosity probably would have left it at that, content with the previous revelation's absurdity. A man of lesser curiosity probably would have been hesitant to delve deeper into the psyche of someone who had proudly delivered the previous statement as if it were some kind of toughness merit badge.

But a man of lesser curiosity Leach is not, and he continued to poke his golden goose of unintentional comedy for bonus eggs. "Did you ever have to stick an olive up your ass and then eat it?" Leach inquired with the earnestness of a funeral director.

"No," retorted Moot, as if Leach's suggestion was somehow more offensive than the image of being nude in a tub with another grown man while slugging raw eggs and beers to the point of regurgitation.

Leach nodded his head and squinted as other great acts of toughness and Greek brotherhood swirled in his mind. "Did you ever funnel each other's piss like it was a beer?" he asked, continuing his line of questioning in a seemingly sincere effort to determine exactly how tough Moot's undergraduate experience had been.

"No," responded Moot, unsure of where exactly the line of questioning was headed. Leach set his gaze forward and stared through the windshield and thought for a moment. "So then, other than the tub it was pretty much just paddles and, 'Thank you, sir, may I have another?'" concluded the Pepperdine-trained lawyer, matter-of-factly.

"Shut the #%&* up," said Moot, indicating that the discussion had come to a conclusion. He looked back over the steering wheel and the thousands of miles of dark road ahead of them. And so it went for the curious instigator and the oblivious court jester as they drove across the Bible Belt all the way to Florida and back again, picking up recruits to come join the aerial revolution in Mount Pleasant along the way.

The Abbott-and-Costello routines that took place between Leach and Moot weren't limited to the time they shared on the road. One evening, Moot rolled along as the fifth wheel on a double date with the Mummes and the Leachs to see Kevin Costner as Lieutenant John Dunbar in *Dances with Wolves*. Early in the film, Dunbar is led across the frontier to his post at Fort Sedgewick by a crude wagon driver named Timmons. Along the way, Timmons cracks bad jokes when the two come upon an arrow-riddled skeleton on the prairie. Later in the trip, he unleashes a symphony of bodily functions in Dunbar's direction and laughs, "Put that in your book," before cackling himself to sleep. Exasperated, Dunbar writes in his journal, "Were it not for my companion, I believe I would be having the time of my life. I know he means well, but he is quite possibly the foulest man I have ever met."

Leach empathized with Dunbar right away, having spent three weeks in close quarters with Moot only a few months previously. As Dunbar narrated his writings, Leach leaned forward in his seat so he could look past Sharon, Hal, and June to stare intently at Moot who was sitting on the other end of the group. Moot felt Leach's eyes on him, but continued to look forward nonchalantly to downplay the fact that he was currently being compared to the foulest man Costner's character had ever met. Unfortunately for Moot, Sharon, Hal, and June picked up on Leach's gaze before they all lost their composure in a fit of laughter.

6

MIDNIGHT MANEUVERS

Fortunately for Iowa Wesleyan's coaching staff, the team's turnaround in 1989 meant that they wouldn't have to assemble another recruiting class almost exclusively with out-of-state talent. The Tigers' high flying offense garnered the admiration of a number of talented prep athletes throughout southeast Iowa. Among the converted was none other than Mount Pleasant's own Dana Holgorsen, the same recruit who refused to leave his English class to speak with Mumme less than a year before.

After a lackluster season at St. Ambrose University where he was the team's leading receiver with twelve catches through nine games before being moved to defensive back, Holgorsen decided it was time for him to head back home. When he returned to Mount Pleasant for Christmas break, he crossed paths with Mumme, Dewald, and a few other members of the high flying Tigers on a couple of occasions and couldn't help but notice that they seemed to be enjoying football a lot more than he was. For the first time that he could remember, people in his hometown seemed genuinely interested in Iowa Wesleyan football. He had been hanging around town for a few weeks before he took a big gulp to swallow his metaphorical pride and headed into Mumme's office to ask for another chance to be part of the Iowa Wesleyan football team.

As unlikely as it may have seemed eleven months previously, Mumme wasn't surprised by Holgorsen's about-face on his football program. Mumme had been following the hometown receiver's season at St. Ambrose through periodic

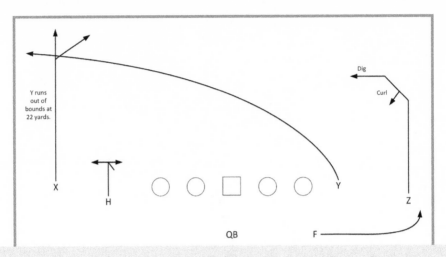

Y runs
out of
bounds at
22 yards.

X

H

QB

F

Y

Z

Dig

Curl

When Dana Holgorsen took over at Z-receiver heading into the 1990 season I learned a valuable lesson about molding the offense to the personnel running it. The player he was replacing—Dereck Hall—did a great job catching the dig route for us during the 1989 season, but when Dana got on campus he had some trouble with it. We found that he caught curls much better, so we changed the Z-receiver's route on our 95 call from a dig to a curl. To me, the lesson was clear: "Don't be afraid to make adjustments."

updates from Holgorsen's high school coach Bob Evans during morning coffee at Dicky's. Around the time he learned that Holgorsen was moved to defensive back, Mumme started to believe that he might get a second chance to add Holgorsen to the roster. The team would need him, too. Wide receiver Chris Edwards had completed his eligibility and would not be returning for the 1990 season and the Tigers were desperately seeking a serviceable replacement. By the time Holgorsen came around to ask for a second chance to play for Iowa Wesleyan, Mumme was so happy to see him that he spared Mount Pleasant's prodigal son his mandatory dish of crow and welcomed him back with open arms.

At the time, Holgorsen explained his change of heart to a local reporter this way: "This is my type of program. They like to throw the ball, and that's what I like to see. They've got a great quarterback in Dustin and an outstanding line. This program really has really changed. It wasn't like this at all when I graduated from high school. I don't think I would have even considered Wesleyan then. Now, this is the program that I want to be in and Coach Mumme is the guy I want to play for."

Holgorsen wasn't the only Mount Pleasant product that was excited about the vast improvement he was seeing in his hometown team. In the winter of 1990,

Charlie Moot was in hot pursuit of Mount Pleasant High School product and all-state linebacker Marc Hill. In the end, Moot was able to sell Hill on Iowa Wesleyan's gridiron revival, and Hill decided to get involved in the turnaround right away instead of spending a season of misery away from his hometown. When he signed his letter of intent, Hill explained his choice this way: "I think the program is really in the early stages and I'm excited to be part of the building process. They showed last year that they could win some games and I think we'll be winning next year."

Both local products figured to see a good deal of playing time during the upcoming season. They were joined by a half dozen other recruits from southeast Iowa—twice the number that chose to come to Iowa Wesleyan a year before—and thirty-five other players from across the country who wanted to be a part of what was happening at Iowa Wesleyan. Most of the athletes who chose to play for the Tigers hadn't arrived at that decision on their own like Holgorsen did. In a number of instances, chances were that Mike Leach played some role in getting them to Mount Pleasant.

Two such players were Bill Bedenbaugh and York Kurinsky, a pair of close friends who played on the offensive line together at St. Charles High School in Illinois. Bedenbaugh played center and was lured to Mount Pleasant by the Tigers' quirky offensive line coach. Early on in the recruitment cycle it became clear to Bedenbaugh that Iowa Wesleyan was his best option for continuing his football career. He wasn't being heavily recruited elsewhere, but that didn't stop Leach from calling Bedenbaugh at all hours of the night to talk football or whatever else happened to be on his mind, usually the latter. "I knew playing for Leach would be interesting," Bedenbaugh said of his recruitment.

Bedenbaugh was a gritty player and a great addition to Iowa Wesleyan's roster, but it's fair to say that Kurinsky was the real prize of the two recruits. Kurinsky was a six-foot, four-inch, 245-pound offensive tackle who was coveted by a number of Big 10 offensive line coaches. Iowa Wesleyan didn't seem to have much of a chance of landing the prized recruit, but the odds didn't matter to Leach. He was determined to have Kurinsky join his offensive line come fall, and he was willing to accomplish that goal by any means necessary. Fortunately for Leach, Kurinsky hadn't fared well on his SATs, and his score on the test left him ineligible to play NCAA football in the fall of 1990.

By the time he was recruiting York, Mike already appreciated the benefits of lining up his offensive line in wide splits. The wider gaps create bigger passing lanes and escape routes for quarterbacks and move the defensive end, usually the opposition's best pass rusher, further from the quarterback. Larger gaps can also isolate the offensive linemen, leaving the best lineman as a one-on-one pass blocker. We needed an athletic left tackle to make it work, and York definitely fit the bill. Mike worked really hard to get him and thankfully that work ultimately paid off.

Frustrated, Kurinsky decided that his best chance of getting eligible would be to take the ACT, an alternative standardized test, and score high enough to have the NCAA waive the SAT minimum requirement. Before that could happen, Leach managed to talk Kurinsky into coming to Iowa Wesleyan to visit the campus along with Bedenbaugh to get a feel for what life would be like as a member of the Tigers. For their first night on campus, Kurinsky and Bedenbaugh spent the evening out and about with rising seniors John Coneset and Andrew Przybylski.

Although details of the evening's events remain a well-guarded secret, Kurinsky and Bedenbaugh showed up in the coaches' offices the following morning with glassy eyes and goofy grins before they headed home. When Mumme walked into the office, the two of them jumped to attention. Taken back by their eagerness, Mumme smirked and asked, "How'd you like Iowa Wesleyan?"

Almost in unison, Bedenbaugh and Kurinsky quickly exclaimed, "This is the greatest place we've ever been!" Mumme was surprised and thought to himself that no one had ever said such a thing about Iowa Wesleyan before, but managed to avoid tipping his hand as the odor of stale beer hung in the room like a fog. The conversation lasted a bit longer before Mumme thanked them for coming to campus and expressed his desire for them to return to Mount Pleasant in August for training camp. Both players agreed that they would be there.

After the trip, Kurinsky was smitten with the idea of playing for a program and a coaching staff that he believed to be on the rise. Because it was late in recruiting season and most scholarships the team had to offer had been taken up, Mumme was forced to lowball his prize recruit with a partial scholarship when he went to Illinois to make Kurinsky's decision to play at Iowa Wesleyan official.

Kurinsky's father wasn't nearly as impressed as his son was with the prospect of playing in the NAIA on a partial scholarship, and a disagreement began to escalate at the Kurinskys' kitchen table when Mumme presented a letter of intent for York to sign. For this particular decision, Mumme found himself to be more of a deer in the headlights than a lobbyist as he watched father and son argue over York's future. Fortunately, Mumme learned that Leach's sales pitch had stuck when the younger Kurinsky finally grabbed a pen and shouted, "I'm going to Iowa Wesleyan, Dad." He quickly scribbled his signature on the letter of intent, dropped the pen on the table and looked at his father and said, "I'm going to play for Coach Mumme and Coach Leach." Mumme immediately collected the necessary paperwork and got the hell out of there.

The Tigers' roster also experienced addition through subtraction during the offseason. Recruiting had taken place at such a fever pitch leading up to the 1989 season that the coaching staff didn't have the time to do a thorough character evaluation of all their recruits as they built the roster. Every now and then, a player they had brought to campus made the coaching staff lament their inability to perform their due diligence in the recruiting cycle. One instance of buyer's remorse came when Mike Jefferson ended his playing career at Iowa Wesleyan by performing a striptease and leaving his equipment behind like a trail of bread crumbs in the middle of the Central Methodist game. Another played out in the saga of a cornerback by the name of Jimmy Korn.

Korn was a cornerback out of Fort Scott Community College in Kansas City who ran a 4.4-second forty-yard dash and played a position that Mumme was desperate to fill. When he arrived at Iowa Wesleyan's 1989 preseason camp, it quickly became apparent that Korn primarily used that speed to track down opposing receivers that he had just allowed to catch the football. Korn couldn't quite grasp his responsibilities when it came to being a member of a defensive unit or a member of polite society and had a knack for being in the wrong place at the wrong time both on and off the field.

The transgression that stamped Korn's ticket out of Mount Pleasant began when he moseyed into student assistant Mike Bontrager's dorm room to inform Bontrager that he would be "borrowing" his phone card. Bontrager, a dedicated member of the team's support staff as well as the owner of a glaucoma patient's eye prescription and jellyfish's backbone, quietly acquiesced and allowed Korn to take his phone card without much of a protest. A month later Bontrager received a $400 bill in the mail for the phone card and went to Korn's dorm to request that he be reimbursed. Korn dismissed Bontrager as quickly as he would a visit from Jehovah's Witnesses on New Year's morning.

Short on options, Bontrager brought the bill to Mumme's office to explain the situation and gain the coach's intervention. Mumme took a look at the phone bill and noticed that the vast majority of the calls had been made to numbers with a Kansas City area code, so he began calling those numbers to see if they knew anyone at Iowa Wesleyan. Mumme wound up spending his afternoon speaking with a gaggle of scorned women who were supremely pissed at Korn.

After he gathered the information that he needed, Mumme called Korn to his office to discuss the matter of the Bontrager's phone card. He informed Korn that he would be paying back Bontrager for every cent on the phone card bill before he would be allowed to rejoin the program. Korn made a frivolous effort to use the "It wasn't me" defense before Mumme cut him off, informed him that he'd spoken with Korn's ex-girlfriends, and that he didn't want to hear it. He ended the meeting with a decree: "You stole Bontrager's phone card, you're going to pay him back, or I'm going to kick you off the team."

Korn spent the next few weeks raising the necessary funds to reimburse Bontrager for his use of the phone card bit by bit. On delivering the final installment of reimbursement pay plan, he issued a final piece of advice to Bontrager: "If you ever tell coach anything I've done ever again, I'll kill you." A flustered and petrified Bontrager immediately brought the news to Mumme's office.

Again, Mumme called Korn to his office. This time he opted not to extend an opportunity for penance and informed his former player that he wouldn't be receiving a uniform for spring practice because he was no longer part of the team. Korn immediately protested that Mumme had told him that he could rejoin the team when he repaid his debt to Bontrager. Not in the mood to engage in a debate and weary of triggering the murder clause in Korn's threat to Bontrager, Mumme simply snarled, "I lied. How's it feel?" With that, Korn got up, flipped over his chair, and swore his way out of Mumme's office.

Mumme ran his hands through his hair and let out a sigh of relief, comforted by the knowledge that he was done dealing with Korn as a football player. However, a few moments later it began to sink in that he had just double-crossed a criminal who knew exactly where his family lived. Mumme quickly picked up the phone to call June and inquire about the whereabouts of their youngest daughter Leslie. "She's outside playing," responded his wife. Mumme calmly told his wife that it might be better if Leslie came in for the time being and played inside for the next couple days. Fortunately, Korn's dismissal was the last that Mumme or the team would hear of him, and after a week or so, Leslie was free to resume playing in the backyard.

Although the process was painful, pruning some of the thornier branches of Iowa Wesleyan's football team during the winter of 1990 allowed for tremendous growth on the part of the players that remained on campus. Dismissing players such as Korn and Jefferson eliminated a number of distractions and allowed the remaining players on the roster to keep their focus squarely on football, which was easy, because there wasn't much else to do in Mount Pleasant. Iowa Wesleyan didn't boast great facilities or a strong football tradition. Campus was located nowhere near anything that resembled a major city and it wasn't exactly inundated with beautiful co-eds. The Tigers who survived the pruning process following the 1989 season shared one interest: they wanted to be better football players. That common thread led the team to make strides during the offseason that would prove to be monumental in Iowa Wesleyan's on-field success as well as the evolution of Mumme's fledgling offensive system.

The NAIA allowed coaches to work with their players throughout the offseason, an opportunity that Mumme exploited to the fullest in a campus gymnasium late Tuesday and Thursday nights throughout the cold Iowa Winter. Practicing late at night was a matter of necessity rather than of preference because 11:30 to 12:30 happened to be the only time that the gym was available to the football team. Although the gym provided a limited timeframe and a limited space for the team to work out, the facilities provided the means to meet Mumme's goals and the team's needs. The stripped down practice sessions that took place in the gym throughout the winter came to be known as Midnight Maneuvers.

When pressed as to why the Eagles were such a great band, Don Henley once said that it probably had something to do with the band's "great capacity for boredom." The same is true for our offense. In practice we ceaselessly repeat the skills our players will use in games so that those skills become second nature. A bad snap made me realize that we needed to spend a winter in the gym getting it right before we could consistently execute it in the game.

Midnight Maneuvers was little more than a basic series of conditioning exercises, agility drills, and repetition of gridiron fundamentals that didn't require a whole lot of space. The biggest development that came out of Midnight Maneuvers was Iowa Wesleyan's mastery of the shotgun snap, which Mumme had attempted to include in the Tigers' repertoire during the 1989 season with little success. After the Tigers dropped the shootout with Greenville College, Mumme got to thinking that Dewald could be more effective taking snaps out of the shotgun, so he added the formation to the following week's game plan. University of Chicago figured to be a less competitive opponent than Greenville, and the game provided the ideal occasion to take the shotgun snap for a test drive. It didn't take long for Mumme to reconsider the implementation of the midseason wrinkle.

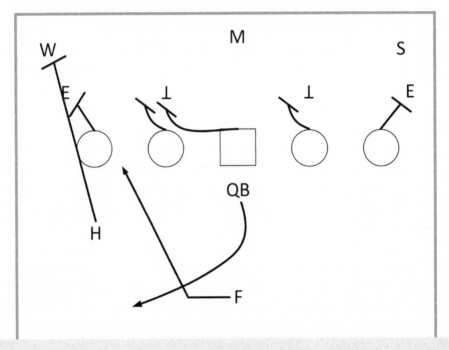

When we went to the shotgun before the 1990 season we had to adjust our running game to accommodate the new formation. Our lead play was 35, and the diagrams illustrate the changes that we had to make. The first diagram shows how we ran 35 from our Brown right set during the 1989 season.

On the game's first play, Dewald lined up 5 yards behind Coneset, surveyed the defense, barked out a cadence, and called for a snap that was promptly launched six feet over his head and about 90 feet behind him. This led to Dewald sprinting 30 yards back in a frantic effort to track down the errant snap before he pounced on the ball for a 35-yard loss. When the rest of the offense finally caught up with their quarterback and formed a huddle, a winded, disheveled, and annoyed Dewald began calling the next play, before thinking better of it and asking

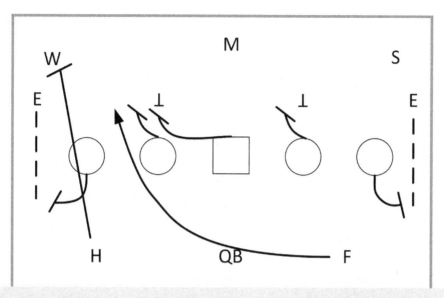

This diagram illustrates how we ran the same play out of the shotgun formation during the 1991 season.

Coneset, "So, John, do you have any plays for second and 45?" Recognizing the rhetorical nature of the inquiry, Coneset remained mute and listened for the plan of attack for second down. His silence didn't last.

When the huddle broke, Coneset walked up to the line of scrimmage, turned around to look at his quarterback and shouted "%&*# you!" before getting into his stance. Despite the early miscue, Wesleyan managed to regroup and post a 25-point win. Nonetheless, for the sake of the offense's continued prosperity, not to mention team chemistry, Mumme chose to table the shotgun formation until the offseason.

The ceaseless repetition that took place during Midnight Maneuvers made delivering and receiving the shotgun snap second nature for Iowa Wesleyan's centers and quarterbacks, turning a major question mark into one of the team's strengths in the process. Ultimately, the approach that the team took to perfecting the shotgun snap during the winter of 1990 became something of a blueprint for practices within Mumme's offensive system from that point forward. His team's mastery of the shotgun led Mumme to embrace the idea of mastering a few skills rather than seeking to simply be decent at lots of different skills. The philosophy behind this approach was the idea that it is better for a team to be great at the few things it attempts to do on the field rather than attempt to do everything.

"You know, football is a lot like life," Mumme commented to a reporter early in his time at Iowa Wesleyan. "You just can't be good at everything. You've got to pick what you do best and just go with it." Anyone who has eaten a mediocre meal at a restaurant with a fourteen-page menu would agree.

Iowa Wesleyan's foray into the shotgun snap also constituted the first steps that Mumme took toward creating his own offense. During his tenure at Copperas Cove and his first year at Iowa Wesleyan, Mumme essentially ran a carbon copy of the offense that he watched LaVell Edwards run at BYU. Installing the shotgun snap represented his first major tweak to the offensive approach that he had relied on for all of his previous success. The shotgun snap wouldn't be his final adjustment to the offense before the 1990 season.

As Mumme and Leach tinkered with the offense at Iowa Wesleyan, they were fond of saying "build a better mousetrap and the world will beat a path to your door" to one another. The sentiment behind the expression captured the essence of what they were trying to accomplish with their perpetual tinkering of their system, which was a superior offensive scheme.

The driving factor behind Mumme and Leach's endless endeavor to innovate was a shared innate and indiscriminate curiosity. That inquisitiveness took them to a variety of destinations as they searched for parts to a superior mousetrap. They may have been pioneering a new offensive system, but they weren't alone in their efforts to elevate the place of the passing game in the pursuit of points. Just about everywhere they looked there were other coaches developing new approaches to the passing game. "It was a pretty good time football-wise for some level of innovation," recalled Leach of his and Mumme's efforts to take the Tigers' offense to the next level. "There were lots of guys experimenting and throwing the ball effectively to draw ideas from."

The NFL had been dominated by the San Francisco 49ers in the 1980s, and head coach Bill Walsh's West Coast offense was gaining traction among football coaches across the country. Most importantly, Walsh's success proliferated a belief in coaching circles that a football team could be successful by taking a more cerebral approach to a game that had been dominated by a ground-oriented smash-mouth approach since its inception. Run-and-shoot pioneer and Walsh inspiration Mouse Davis found mainstream acceptance when he became the Detroit Lions' offensive coordinator in 1988. University of Houston offensive coordinator John

Jenkins's installation of the run-and-shoot earned Cougars' quarterback Andre Ware a Heisman Trophy in 1989. Jenkins was named the Cougars' head coach before the 1990 season when former head coach Jack Pardee left to take over the same post with the Houston Oilers. Meanwhile, Edwards' BYU teams continued to execute its drop back passing offense with great success.

As many places as there were to gather ideas from, Mumme and Leach had little trouble focusing in on the things different teams were doing that would translate successfully to Iowa Wesleyan's existing system and personnel. "One thing we always embraced was having the discipline to make choices and lock into certain things so that we could develop our skills and do it as effectively as possible," Leach said of his and Mumme's ability to choose the best components for their offense.

However, Mumme was already confident in the package of offensive plays that he had put together. "We weren't looking for schemes and plays," he recalls of the pilgrimages he and Leach made in the beginning of 1990. "We were looking for the best way to teach fundamentals."

As the offseason moved along, it became clear that that Mumme and Leach weren't the only ones who were reconsidering the direction of the program for the 1990 season. The dozens of scheduling requests that greeted Mumme little more than a year before had been replaced by calls from scheduled opponents informing him that they weren't interested in playing Iowa Wesleyan in 1990. University of Dubuque and Culver Stockton College, the first two opponents on the schedule, cancelled and left Iowa Wesleyan scrambling to fill the open dates.

To make matters worse, when Mumme and athletic director David Johnsen arrived at the Illini-Badger-Hawkeye Conference Meeting in Chicago in March, they were greeted with a motion to dismiss Iowa Wesleyan from the league. Some of the grumbling that came from those supporting the measure alleged that the Tigers were giving away too many football scholarships. It was a puzzling accusation, especially considering the fact that neither the NAIA nor the league had any rules that stipulated the number of scholarships a team could award. It's more likely that those voting in the affirmative were salty over the fact that a team they expected to be a patsy finished second in the league and hung 38 points a game on conference opponents. They weren't interested in another season of winding up on the losing end of lopsided scores. In the end, the ayes had it, and Iowa Wesleyan was left with one season to exact revenge on the league that was discarding it.

York Kurinsky (77) and Jaime Luera (76) jog to the sidelines at Mapeleaf Field.

1989 Iowa Wesleyan football team photo.

Hal Mumme coaches Dustin Dewald during a 1989 home game.

Andrew Przybylski (65) and John Coneset (50) just two blazers
away from pulling off a passable Crockett and Tubbs.

Shawn Martin (78), Andrew Przybylski (65), John Coneset (50), Robert Draper (66), and
Dennis Gatewood (61) pose at the Victory Bell on Iowa Wesleyan's campus. The bell is
rung to celebrate victories and great occasions.

Hometown boys Marc Hill (*left*) and Dana Holgorsen (*right*) pose with Mount Pleasant
Mayor Tom Vilsack, now the US Secretary of Agriculture.

Mike Leach coaches the offensive line at Mapleleaf Field.

Dustin Dewald (16) and Hal Mumme (*far right*) pose with Olivet Nazarene's head coach and quarterback after the second Steamboat Classic.

Bruce Carter (1), Dana Holgorsen (22), and Dustin Dewald (16) taking things
literally before the 1991 season.

7

OPPONENTS EVERYWHERE

The Iowa Wesleyan Tigers came into the 1990 season with heightened expectations swirling all around them. Some of those expectations came from within a team that had a good idea of how well they were capable of performing. They had lofty goals for their season. Others came from outsiders who had seen Mumme's offense put up 37 points a game on 347 yards passing over the course of a season that was seven points away from perfection.

Within the Tigers' locker room, the goals for Mumme's second season were clear, and he had no problem sharing them with anyone who was willing to listen. "First of all, we want to win our conference. Secondly, we want to make the playoffs and third, we want to have fun playing this game." A league championship certainly seemed within the Tigers reach, especially considering the fact that they were returning twenty-one starters from a team that had missed out on the 1989 Illini-Badger-Hawkeye Conference title by the slimmest of margins. Three of those returning starters—Dustin Dewald, Andrew Przybylski, and Dennis Gatewood—were named to the NAIA's preseason Academic All-American team. *College Football Preview* magazine thought so highly of Dewald and his supporting cast that the publication named him a preseason All-American and ranked the team eleventh in the nation among NAIA Division II teams in 1990's preseason poll.

However, not everyone shared *College Football Preview's* enthusiasm for the upcoming season. Some of the team's staunchest adversaries were those who had been closest to the Tigers before Mumme's tenure as head coach. Traditional opponents had grown accustomed to the program's competitive indifference, and they were none too pleased with the gridiron rejuvenation in Mount Pleasant. Conversely, administrators at Iowa Wesleyan outside of the athletic department were dismayed with the institution's increased commitment to the success of its football program. As Mark Twain put it, "Be good and you will be lonesome." After only one season at the helm for Iowa Wesleyan, Mumme was fixing to become one of the loneliest men in southeast Iowa.

Dubuque, Culver-Stockton, Grinnell, Chicago, Central Methodist, and Trinity all chose to cancel scheduled games with Iowa Wesleyan. The year before Mumme was frantically searching for players to fill out the Tigers' roster. This year, he was frantically searching for teams that actually had the mettle to face off against his squad, leaving two unfavorable options for filling the gaping holes in the schedule for the upcoming season. On the one hand, Mumme could trim the Tigers' schedule to eight or nine games. Most other teams already had full schedules for the 1990 season, and finding an NAIA team in the Midwest that was willing to tangle with Iowa Wesleyan's offense was proving to be an impossible endeavor. If Mumme wanted to give his players a full schedule of games for the fall of 1990, he was going to have to look outside of Iowa Wesleyan's geographic and competitive comfort zone for opponents.

Portland State University and Morningside College, two NCAA Division II programs, expressed interest in playing the Tigers in 1990. Mumme saw the games as an opportunity for Iowa Wesleyan football to begin moving forward and competitively realign itself to continue attracting quality recruits to Mount Pleasant. He felt that Iowa Wesleyan should ultimately compete at the NCAA Division II level to capitalize on recent success and build a better football team. Presented with the option for the program to grow or decay, the choice was obvious to Mumme and Iowa Wesleyan's administration. Unfortunately, they disagreed on what that choice should have been.

The old guard on campus was quite fond of the way the school had been doing things on the gridiron for the past ninety-three years. Iowa Wesleyan's football team competed against Midwestern schools with a roster full of Midwestern kids because that's the way things had always been done in Mount Pleasant. Football was given the same amount of attention as any other extracurricular activity on campus, and nobody much cared about the results, even if the old way of doing things was yielding results that could objectively be classified as second rate.

74

On the other hand, it was Mumme's job to care about the results, and he would have his team line up against Notre Dame before he would put a competitive straight jacket on them. His team spent the 1989 season proving that they were capable of playing at a higher level, and he intended to give them that opportunity. Naturally, Mumme went ahead and put three games with NCAA Division II opponents on the schedule despite objections from some of the senior members of Iowa Wesleyan's administration. In doing so, each one of those contests became a de facto referendum on the wisdom of the Tigers eventually joining their ranks. The line in the sand had been drawn between Mumme's vision for the future of Iowa Wesleyan football and the old guard's esteem for the program's tradition of mediocrity.

The news of games with NCAA Division II opponents was also met with some resistance by the coaching staff initially, particularly Charlie Moot. When Mumme informed Moot and Mike Leach that Iowa Wesleyan would be adding Portland State—the top-ranked team in the nation among its NCAA peers—to the schedule, Moot nearly gave himself an aneurysm. Leach didn't say much; he just kept his eyes on Moot, riveted by his colleague's reaction. When Moot finally managed to string together a coherent sentence, he inquired how in the world Mumme expected his defense to compete against that sort of opponent.

Mumme decided to justify the schedule by taking the economic route. He calmly responded, "You've got a point, Charlie. But they're reimbursing our travel expenses and paying us $10,000 on top of that for the game. So here's what we can do: we can cancel the game with Portland State and not get $10,000. In which case I can just head down to Dr. Prins' office and he can take it out of your salaries." Suddenly, the game with Portland State became a brilliant idea to Moot, and he began suggesting other opponents Iowa Wesleyan could play to get even more money. At that point, a home-and-home with University of Iowa probably wouldn't have been out of the question.

With the rest of the coaching staff on board to play a more competitive schedule and each side of the debate firmly entrenched in their respective bunkers, the Tigers began the 1990 season with a trip to Sioux City to tangle with NCAA Division II opponent Morningside College. Despite the difference between the two teams' competitive alliances, Iowa Wesleyan entered the game feeling pretty good about its chances to come away with a victory. Morningside posted a dismal record of 2–9 the previous season and the film that the Tigers watched of their opponent was equally unimpressive. It wasn't long after opening kickoff that the players realized that Morningside had essentially cleaned house in the offseason and marched out a new and vastly improved roster.

From the contest's outset it was clear that Iowa Wesleyan was outmatched, particularly at the line of scrimmage. Morningside had strong offensive and defensive lines that held the type of physical advantage one might expect from a team that competed at a higher level. Consequently, Dewald spent most of his afternoon rushing his throws and ducking for cover, completing only 11 of 33 passes for 139 yards in the process. The Tigers could only manage to grind out a measly 20 yards on the ground as they posted just three points on the afternoon. The effort was good for the feeblest offensive output of Mumme's tenure to date.

Defensively the Tigers had their hands full as well. Again at a disadvantage on the line of scrimmage, Morningside had its way with Iowa Wesleyan's defense, rushing for 361 yards and throwing for another 170 en route to a 55–3 victory.

Things didn't figure to get any easier the following week when the Tigers traveled to Oregon to face off against Portland State University, another NCAA Division II opponent and the top-ranked team in the country at that level. However, the nearly two thousand-mile trip from Mount Pleasant to Portland presented a rare treat for much of Iowa Wesleyan's roster: the opportunity to fly. It was the first flight for many of the players on Iowa Wesleyan's roster, and they crowded the windows of the airplane to catch an aerial view of the Rocky Mountains and snap a few photographs of the scenery below. Mumme chuckled as he sat in front of the aircraft and heard the excited voices and camera clicks sounding off behind him; he knew there wasn't a photo developer on the planet that would be able to get those pictures to come out in focus.

The results of the ensuing game would do little to alleviate any of the disappointment the players would feel when they picked up their prints. Again, Iowa Wesleyan was undersized and overmatched at the line of scrimmage and struggled to hang with another physically superior opponent. Dewald threw 45 passes, the vast majority of them under heavy duress, completing only 18 of them for 91 yards and an interception. Things didn't go any better on the ground as the Tigers labored for 33 yards on 18 carries. Meanwhile, the Vikings ran for 297 yards, passed for 278, and cruised to a 40–3 victory.

The second blowout loss to start the season gave Mumme's opponents in the administration all the ammunition that they needed to shoot down the notion that Tiger football could compete on a higher level. Before the season, Dr. Robert Prins put together a committee whose purpose was to explore the possibility of

Iowa Wesleyan football making the jump to the NCAA Division II level. Early meetings generally consisted of Mumme laying out how the heightened level of competition would attract more quality recruits to Mount Pleasant and raise the profile of the school. The standard response to these ideas was headshakes from the other committee members before one of them would ask, "Why would we want to do that?" For those who were against the move in the first place, the Morningside and Portland State losses provided all the answers that they needed as to why the school wasn't interested in moving up to compete in the NCAA Division II. As an added bonus, Mumme now got to hear committee members fire off snarky comments at meetings instead of their usual routine of feigning ignorance.

As poorly as the results of the season's first two games had been and as miserable as those committee meetings became, the proverbial storm clouds of a cumulative season scoreboard of 95–6 over the first two games weren't without silver linings. The speed of the NCCA Division II game was significantly faster than what the Tigers would see from any of their NAIA opponents, and after six quarters at that pace, the team began to adjust to the heightened level of play. It showed defensively, as Moot's unit surrendered only one touchdown in the second half of the Portland State game after giving up 33 points in the first half. If nothing else, the resolve the team showed over the course of two brutal games was encouraging to the coaching staff. "Our guys had a lot of fight in them the second half," commented Mumme after the game. "At halftime they wanted to get back out there and play. I think if you asked them at the end of the game if they wanted to play more, they would have said yes."

Mumme hadn't only gathered valuable information about his team's mental makeup during the Tigers' drubbing in the season's first eight quarters; he and his staff learned some valuable coaching lessons along the way. For one, Leach had to reevaluate the blocking schemes he was implementing to protect the quarterback. The passing game struggled mightily in the first two games of the season, and that was primarily a result of Iowa Wesleyan's offensive line being physically overwhelmed by their opponents on the defensive line. Leach figured that his best bet to compete with a physically limited offensive line was to use the dimensions of the field. Mumme and Leach both believed in using large splits on the offensive line to isolate defensive linemen, a strategy they initially adopted from BYU. Wider splits also put more space between the defensive end (usually the team's best pass rusher) and the quarterback while providing a shorter passer like Dewald with wider passing lanes to throw the ball through. This strategy became even more pronounced as Leach labored to make his offensive line effective against their more physical NCAA Division II opponents.

Then there was the lone bright spot of Iowa Wesleyan's opening day pummeling against Morningside, which was the only scoring drive the offense managed to put together after successfully executing a fake punt on fourth and long deep in their own territory. The lesson of the fake punt's success wasn't lost on Mumme. "It was kind of a desperate move, but it's one that's pretty easy to get away with. Later on it became something we did on a regular basis." There's nothing more dangerous than someone with nothing to lose. Starting that bleak afternoon in Sioux City, Mumme decided that his team would be a threat each and every down that it had the ball, whether or not the offense was on the field.

It was a ploy that drew exasperated sighs from defensive coordinators everywhere, both from those coaching against the Tigers as well as those standing alongside Mumme on the Iowa Wesleyan sideline. Whether or not future attempts to pull a fast one on a snoozing special teams unit proved successful, it was a move that opponents needed to account for in the week of practice leading up to the game. The constant threat of a fake punt also fit nicely into a gridiron philosophy that sought to challenge conventional wisdom and aggressively pursue all of the opportunities that the playing field and the rulebook had to offer.

The coaches weren't the only ones to make improvements as a result of the fierce competition provided by the first two games of the season, the players did as well. The team hadn't played any opponents of Morningside or Portland State's caliber the previous season, and the glimpse those games provided into what it took to compete on the NCAA Division II level proved to be a strong motivator for the team during offseason workouts. The heightened intensity during the offseason would go on to pay enormous dividends in the 1991 season when Iowa Wesleyan moved up to NAIA Division I and once again had NCAA Division II opponents on its schedule.

Furthermore, refining his already quick release time in the pocket became a point of improvement for Dewald. He'd struggled through eight quarters of trying to elude defensive linemen that were stronger and faster than those that he had seen the previous year. Instead of avoiding would-be tacklers by trying to outrun them, Dewald focused on hitting receivers on hot routes as quickly as possible when he felt the pocket around him collapsing. By the end of the season, Iowa Wesleyan's offense was sending a hot route on every play instead of leaving additional blockers in the backfield because Dewald was so comfortable and effective getting the ball to his check down receivers in a hurry.

After two weeks of rugged competition, the Tigers began squaring off against teams that competed at their level with varying results. Iowa Wesleyan ran away with its first game against an NAIA opponent, a 38–14 victory at Midwestern State University. The following week, questionable officiating stalled six of the Tigers' twelve offensive drives, and the team lost to Lindenwood College, 35–21 in Missouri. A week later, Dewald fully returned to form as he and the team hung 65 points on Concordia University in Chicago to complete the season opening five-game road trip.

Despite their record of 2–3, Iowa Wesleyan was feeling good about a number of things heading into their first home game of the season, a grudge match against Greenville College at Mapleleaf Field. The Tigers were starting to gel offensively and entered the game with the nation's fourth-ranked passing attack. Dewald was averaging more than 350 yards through the air in the three games following the disasters at Morningside and Portland State, and he was beginning to find his rhythm with wide receivers Bruce Carter and Dana Holgorsen, both of whom were in the midst of their first seasons with the team.

Defensively, Mount Pleasant High School product Marc Hill was emerging as a force at linebacker after starting the season on the special teams unit and second on the Tigers' depth chart. Through five games Hill was leading the team with fifty-two tackles and his unexpected play was helping to fill some of the holes left by a number of injuries the Tigers' starters endured over the first five games. Nonetheless, there was a fair amount of concern in Mount Pleasant over how the defense would fair against a team that it had given up 47 points to a year before. To make matters worse, Greenville's vaunted rushing attack was again ranked among the nation's ten best coming into the game.

Despite a shaky start to the 1990 campaign, the Tiger faithful came out in droves to Mapleleaf field for Iowa Wesleyan's home opener, a far cry from the mass exodus that took place after the chili cook-off that preceded the 1989 contest with Greenville. The crowd wasn't disappointed, at least early on. The Tigers looked to be in control of the game for much of the first half, scoring on a 24-yard field goal in the first quarter and tacking on a touchdown early in the second when Dewald connected with Hall from 12 yards out. Greenville quickly roared back with two touchdowns of their own to take a 14–9 lead into the half.

After the intermission, Greenville head coach and Mumme nemesis Max Bowman employed a conservative "bend-but-don't-break" defensive approach that managed to contain the Tiger passing game in the second half. Dewald and the rest of the offense managed to score only 9 points the rest of the way, thanks to a stingy Greenville defense that led to a number of overthrows and dropped balls. Meanwhile, Greenville's offense tallied three more touchdowns en route to a 35–18 victory.

The loss dropped Iowa Wesleyan's record to a disappointing 2–4 for the season. Although the team's record wasn't what the Tigers had in mind when the season began, all was not lost for the embattled squad. Iowa Wesleyan was 1–1 in the Illini-Badger-Hawkeye Conference, and thanks to Greenville's loss to Concordia the week before, the team could still guarantee themselves at least a share of the league title if they could find a way to win the remaining five games on their schedule.

The next week Iowa Wesleyan got back on track with a 38–13 win over Lakeland College at Mapleleaf Field. Seven days later, Dewald and the Tigers reached .500 for the first time all season as they treated visiting MacMurray College to a record shattering 65–14 beat down. Wide receiver Bruce Carter reeled in a school record 16 passes for 156 yards on the day and added an 87-yard kickoff return for a touchdown. It was all part of a surgical afternoon for Dewald, as he cut up MacMurray's defense with 36 completions on 42 attempts for 418 yards and four touchdowns. His 86 percent completion rate on the day was good for the most accurate performance by a passer in school history.

Iowa's defense played hungry as well. Hill recorded five solo tackles and thirteen assists as Wesleyan's defense held MacMurray to a single touchdown until the game's final play, an encouraging sign considering that a number of starters were sidelined with injuries.

After finding their stride against MacMurray, the Tigers looked to record their third consecutive victory when they hosted Eureka College, a team tied with Iowa Wesleyan for second place in the conference. Eureka also boasted the league's best-scoring defense. Nonetheless, Dewald and the offense managed to put up five touchdowns on their way to a 38–21 victory that Mumme described as "winning ugly."

An inconsistent effort on both sides of the ball left Mumme concerned going into a potential trap game with lowly Blackburn College. Despite being winless in conference play, Blackburn had a potent offense that hung 35 points on Greenville and 38 points on Lakeland in their previous two games. Naturally, Mumme relied on the maturity of his starting quarterback to keep the team focused on the step that lied directly ahead. The result was a 57–22 thrashing that set up a showdown with undefeated Concordia for a share of the Illini-Hawkeye-Badger Conference championship. Naturally, the football team's proverbial punch bowl was begging for a metaphorical turd. Iowa Wesleyan's director of public relations was more than happy to complete the analogy.

While Iowa Wesleyan was stringing together its four-game winning streak, Leach, the team's sports information director, was busy making sure that those wins weren't taking place in a vacuum. Saturday evenings after each game, Leach placed phone calls to a number of media outlets and provided a summary of the day's game so that the Sunday newspapers could run a story. Leach was also passing along Dewald's eye-popping numbers to *USA Today* every week, and his stat lines began making regular appearances in the Monday edition's "Weekend's top performances" portion of the sports section. For some reason, all of this positive press for the football team really got under the skin of the school's director of public relations.

She stormed into Leach's office the Monday after the Blackburn game and immediately began admonishing his efforts to spread the word about Iowa Wesleyan football. In an angry tirade laced with the phrase "It's bullshit," she informed Leach that he had overstepped his bounds in bringing Dewald's performance to the attention of *USA Today* and that his calls to the local daily newspapers on Saturday evenings violated the public relations department's protocol for news releases. Standard procedure called for Leach to write a press release and mail it out to the local news outlets on Monday. It didn't matter that the daily papers probably wouldn't run a game story because the press release would be old news by Wednesday, which would be the earliest they could print the story; the procedure made the transmission of news fair to the area's weekly publications.

Her rant struck Leach as being particularly bizarre because he was catching grief for actually doing his job well and bringing positive publicity to the school on a national scale. At some point, Leach had enough and cut off the public relations director so he could deliver his thoughts on the matter. "Iowa Wesleyan sports information has gotten Iowa Wesleyan into *USA Today* three times this year. Your office couldn't get Iowa Wesleyan into *USA Today* unless there was a mass murder on campus." The quip was received about as well as a parking ticket, and the once-angry, now-furious, sports information director stormed out of Leach's office and marched directly to Dr. Prins' to report the transgression.

When Mumme caught wind of the incident from Leach a few minutes later he thought to himself, "Well, that's gonna cause a ripple," and began to mentally prepare his defense for Leach's job in the inevitable showdown with Dr. Prins that he figured was coming his way. The president's reaction wasn't quite as measured. The news of Leach's insubordination immediately sent Prins on the warpath across campus to the football offices, past Sharon Leach who was manning her usual post at the secretary's desk, and into Leach's office where he proceeded to lay into the rogue director of football information. Amid a flurry of castigation, Prins instructed Leach to get out of his office because he was banned from campus for the next three days.

After the dressing down was complete and Dr. Prins went on his way, Leach put on his coat and gathered some personal effects to begin his three days in exile from campus. As he walked out of his office and into the cold November afternoon, he stopped at the secretary's desk and exchanged sheepish glances with Sharon who had a front-row seat for the entire spectacle. Meanwhile, Mumme contemplated how he was going to prepare his team for the biggest game of the year without having his offensive line coach at practice for the next three days.

As for the looming match up with Concordia, Mumme and the rest of the Tigers wanted to win the game badly. Any team with a sense of pride has its sights set on a title when they strap on their pads in August, but this was personal. Iowa Wesleyan's administration almost seemed to resent the team's success, and after learning that they were no longer welcome at the conference meeting back in March, the team knew it had only one season to exact some kind of revenge on the rest of the league. Regardless of the game's outcome, Mumme and the Tigers would be bidding the league farewell with one finger defiantly raised in the air as they rode off into the sunset at the end of the season. Everyone agreed their departure would achieve a greater effect if that finger had a conference championship ring wrapped around it. To drive that point home, the coaching staff had the players sport purple bands on their ring fingers for the week leading up to the Concordia game.

The first half was tightly contested as the Tigers and the Falcons traded touchdowns in the first quarter. Concordia pulled ahead on a 10-yard touchdown run early in the second quarter before Iowa Wesleyan wrestled the lead away with a safety and a 12-yard touchdown pass from Dewald to Bruce Carter. Concordia kicked a 40-yard field goal late in the second quarter to take a 17–15 lead into the half.

Defense dominated the third quarter as both teams failed to put points on the board, setting up a tightly contested fourth quarter to decide the conference championship. Concordia struck first with a long drive that was completed by a 3-yard touchdown run for a 24–15 advantage. Iowa Wesleyan responded with a 17-yard touchdown catch by Hall, but failed to convert the extra point, leaving the score at 24–21 as the clock for the game and the Tigers' season dwindled.

Moot's defense forced Concordia to call on their punt team around midfield with a minute remaining in the game as the offense salivated on the sideline, anxious to start a drive that could bring a conference title back to Mount Pleasant. It wasn't to be. The Falcons ran a fake punt that resulted in a 49-yard touchdown pass and a 31–21 advantage that effectively put the game and a conference championship out of reach. Resilient to the bitter end, the Tigers marched down the field on an existentially heroic drive that ended with Dewald finding Carter for a 3-yard touchdown pass as time expired.

There were plenty of tears in the visitors' locker room in Mequon, Wisconsin, as the Tigers took off their pads and prepared for a long bus ride back to Mount Pleasant. Despite his disappointment, Mumme knew better than to hang is head over the day's result. "I knew that we were going to have a tough year and for these guys to go 6–5 with seven of those games on the road, then I am really proud of them. I'm not apologizing for anything. We played our hearts out. . . . This one hurts more than any of them have all season. It was hard to see it slip away, but I am very proud of these guys. We sat in the locker room like this 10 weeks ago after we'd been beat 95–6 by Morningside and Portland State, and if you'd told me that we'd play seven games on the road and take the number eight team down to the wire like this, then I never would have believed it."

Although the loss left the Tigers without a conference championship and out of the NAIA playoffs, their season wasn't quite over. The afternoon following the loss at Concordia, Iowa Wesleyan was announced as a participant in the Steamboat Bowl along with Olivet Nazarene University of Kankakee, Illinois. The game's continuation indicated success for Mumme at the end of his second season in Mount Pleasant as the wave of local enthusiasm for Iowa Wesleyan football managed to persevere through an up-and-down season. The result was an improved Steamboat Bowl that garnered local sponsorship as well as the distinction of being the nation's only bowl game sanctioned by the NAIA.

That year's edition of the Steamboat Bowl pitted the NAIA's third-ranked passing offense against the nation's best running attack. The game also put Mumme across the field from his former colleague and recruiting partner from his days at the University of Texas at El Paso, Olivet Nazarene head coach Dennis Roland. For the second straight year, the Steamboat Bowl's participants delighted the crowd by lighting up the scoreboard at Burlington's Bracewell

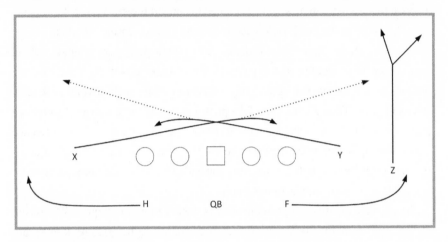

Stadium all afternoon.

Iowa Wesleyan began on the offensive and scored the game's first points thirty-two seconds into the first quarter when Dewald found Holgorsen from 4 yards out. Olivet Nazarene responded with a touchdown of its own early in the second period before the Tigers put up two more touchdowns within a span of twenty-four seconds. The scoring outburst started when Dewald hit Carter in the end zone to cap an eight play, 69-yard drive and continued when Iowa Wesleyan's special teams unit forced a fumble on the ensuing kickoff. After recovering the fumble, Holgorsen reeled in a 30-yard touchdown pass from Dewald on the first play from scrimmage.

Olivet Nazarene looked to be well on their way to digging themselves out of a 21–7 deficit when they drove to Iowa Wesleyan's 1-yard line on fourteen plays to start the second half. On 4th and goal from a yard out, Moot's defense stuffed the nation's best rushing attack for a 1-yard loss and control of the game. From there, Mumme's offense proceeded to drive 98 yards on seven plays for a commanding 27–7 lead. Olivet Nazarene put together a nice comeback effort the rest of the way, but it was too little, too late, and the Tigers emerged from the Steamboat Bowl with a 35–28 victory.

The win put the Iowa Wesleyan's record at 7–5, a respectable tally after the season's 2-4 start. Furthermore, the Tigers were 7–2 against their peers in the NAIA.

Even so, considering the lofty expectations for the 1990 season, the results were a bit of a disappointment. However, the team's effort and resolve in the second half of the season was nothing short of inspiring. The Tigers managed to make it to the postseason for the second straight year as Dewald overcame two lackluster performances to start the season and lead the nation with thirty-three touchdown passes en route to being named a second-team All-American. Carter finished the season with ninety catches, the second best total in the nation. Most importantly, the resilient group had proved its mettle and set the table for a tumultuous 1991 season that would present even more challenges.

8

CHANGES IN LATITUDES, CHANGES IN ATTITUDES

hortly after Mike Leach returned from his 1990 recruiting road trip with Charlie Moot, he headed to Mumme's office to offer his thoughts on the trip and issue a warning to his head coach: "If you ever send me with him again I'll quit." Although the trip with Moot had certainly been amusing at times, there were plenty more that had been mentally exhausting. The last thing Mumme wanted was to lose the services of his offensive line coach, so he shuffled the recruiting pairings for the winter of 1991. Moot wound up flying solo for that year's recruiting trip and Mumme rewarded Leach's endurance of the previous winter's tour by scheduling a trip for the two of them to Key West.

Mumme justified the trip's considerable expense to Dr. Robert Prins by scheduling some recruiting visits, but they could have gone searching for players anywhere. During their time in Mount Pleasant, Leach and Mumme were listening to Jimmy Buffett music constantly. The relaxing vibe of Buffet's ballads about a waterfront life of leisure juxtaposed with the hectic existence of a college football coach surrounded by hundreds of miles of cornfields eased the tension of even the coldest, bleakest days in Iowa. A number of Buffet's songs focused on the laid back, sun-drenched lifestyle that he found in Key West, and at some point they decided that they had to experience it firsthand. Sure, there would be plenty of gridiron components to the trip, but in just as true a sense the trip was about a couple of Parrotheads scoring an all-expenses paid pilgrimage to their Graceland to shoot the breeze for hours as the sun fell from the sky.

The cheapest tickets that Mumme could find were a couple of $500-nonrefundable seats on a flight that flew out of Chicago Midway into Orlando at 7 A.M. Leach would be driving them to the airport, and to make the 250-mile drive and arrive with enough time to park and check-in for their flight, they would need to leave Mount Pleasant no later than 2 A.M.

On the morning of their flight, Mumme woke to his alarm, showered, grabbed his luggage, and walked out to his front porch to minimize the commotion of his departure for his slumbering family. He waited in the frigid darkness for fifteen minutes before heading back inside to call Leach and find out what the holdup was all about. When Mumme dialed Leach's number, he was greeted with a deep, groggy voice on the other end of the line that whispered a startled, "Hello?" Time was of the essence, so Mumme made his point quickly: "Get your ass over here or you're fired!"

Half an hour later Leach's car raced and squealed through Mumme's neighborhood like a getaway car fleeing a crime scene. Mumme tossed his bags into the trunk and sat down in the passenger's seat. Too angry to even look at Leach, Mumme stared straight ahead and reasserted the point that he made over the phone: "If we miss this flight you're fired."

The next three hours were filled with uncomfortable silence while Mumme refused to speak, and Leach raced through hundreds of miles of cornfields in a frantic effort to make it to the airport in time. While Leach drove speeds reserved for stock car racing and feared for his job, Mumme tried to decide whether or not he wanted to see his driver get pulled over. On the one hand, a hefty fine would have served his companion right for being so careless about a trip that Mumme put his neck on the line to make happen. On the other hand, if Leach got pulled over and they missed their flight, the responsibility for explaining their failure to make the flight to Prins would still fall on Mumme. Then he would be forced to give his best assistant the heave-ho to make good on the warning he issued earlier that morning. It was a real pickle.

Somehow, the Richard Petty impression that Leach put on through the cornfields delivered the pair to Chicago Midway in time for their flight. After frantically parking and unloading the car and then sprinting across the parking lot and through the terminal, the two of them made it to their gate with fifteen minutes to spare. Winded and still bitter toward Leach, Mumme flopped into a chair in front of the gate while he waited for the flight attendant to begin boarding passengers. Leach followed suit and pondered how to skillfully break the three hours of tense silence between the two that had begun with his boss threatening to fire him. After a moment, he looked at Mumme with a straight face and offered his best understanding of the situation: "So I take it you're mad."

"That was when I knew I liked Mike Leach," recalled Mumme.

Once the tension was broken by a keen bit of insight on the part of Leach, he and Mumme would enjoy a trip that would go a long way to change the already-revolutionary offense they were running at Iowa Wesleyan.

When the pair arrived in Florida later that afternoon, they headed to the Citrus Bowl to watch the Orlando Thunder of the fledgling World League of American Football work out. Leach had coached under the Thunder's offensive line coach at Cal Poly–San Luis Obispo four years before, but Mumme was there to see Don Matthews. "The Don," as he's known by legions of Canadian Football League fans across the Great White North, had won a Grey Cup with the British Columbia Lions in 1985 but was coming off a rocky season with the Toronto Argonauts that cost him his job and landed him in the World League of American Football.

After practice ended, Mumme and Leach followed the Thunder's coaching staff into the locker room of the Citrus Bowl where Mumme finally got the opportunity to pick Matthews' brain for bits of gridiron wisdom. "Give me your best drill," Mumme requested. In the course of his response, Matthews wound up giving Mumme the drill that his teams used to practice the two-minute offense. Once the film got rolling, Mumme saw "bandit" for the first time. The drill would go on to become a staple of Mumme's teams' practices for the rest of his career.

Bandit was a veritable masterpiece of high-tempo football. Once the ball was set up on the 30-yard line to begin the drill a frenetic fifteen minutes of nonstop football ensued. After each play ended the ball was set up 10 yards from the previous spot for the next snap regardless of the previous play's outcome. There was constant motion. Offensive players sprinted on and off the field between each play. Remaining personnel and substitutions quickly found their spots in the formation and prepared for the next snap while a winded defense desperately tried to align itself properly against a relentless offense and constantly changing personnel. Mumme's eyes lit up as Matthews explained the drill unfolding on film and thought to himself, "Oh, that *is* good." Mumme left the Citrus Bowl settled on the idea that Matthews' bandit drill was something that his team needed to practice every single day.

Before meeting with Matthews, Mumme had been toying with the idea of implementing the no-huddle at Iowa Wesleyan. For one thing, Mumme thought the entertainment value of the no-huddle would be the perfect complement to an offensive system that fans already found to be incredibly engaging. Every football fan knows that the most entertaining part of any televised football game comes during the final two minutes of each half when the offense goes into no-huddle mode and relentlessly runs plays at a weary defense in a last ditch effort to score. How many tense dinner table conversations originated over a husband's insistence that "there are only two minutes left?" However, Mumme's interest in running the no-huddle from opening kick to the final whistle was also tactical. For Mumme, the no-huddle presented another opportunity to build a better mousetrap.

Throughout Mumme's coaching career he'd spent countless hours watching film of teams coached by the likes of Bill Walsh, Mouse Davis, and LaVell Edwards and cherry-picking the plays he found to be most effective. By the time he got to Iowa Wesleyan, Mumme was confident that he had put together a pretty good package of plays. The results he had gotten over the past two seasons obviously supported that conclusion. However, he still believed that the package he had put together could use an edge that would make those plays even more effective on Saturdays. The no-huddle offense seemed to be the perfect wrinkle that would make his evolving offensive system even more of a headache for opposing defensive coordinators, and the coming season seemed to be the perfect opportunity to take that wrinkle for a test drive.

The Tigers had a quarterback in Dustin Dewald who possessed the smarts and the experience required to make the transition. What Mumme didn't have was a thorough understanding of how to effectively practice the no-huddle so that it would translate to game day. Thanks to the film session with Matthews and his explanation of the bandit drill, Mumme had just what he needed. Bandit provided the perfect laboratory to test the offense's ability to execute on the fly and to prepare them for the numerous and often unpredictable situations that would come on game day.

The following day, Mumme and Leach drove 250 miles south to Miami to pay a visit to a promising offensive lineman named Johnny Cherico. Business mixed with pleasure when Cherico's father took Leach and Mumme out on his boat to go fishing. While they were out on the water, the elder Cherico served his guests their first cups of Cuban coffee. Somehow Leach and Mumme failed to get the message that the caffeine content of the Cuban brew was more like espresso as opposed to the cups of coffee they were used to enjoying across from Bob Lamm at Dickey's back in Mount Pleasant. The two of them proceeded to tear through multiple cups on their voyage with Cherico and throw off their sleep cycles for the remainder of the trip.

The next day, still wired from reckless consumption of Cuban coffee, Mumme and Leach hopped in their rental car and headed to Coral Gables. They were hoping to get some time with an assistant coach for the national champion Miami Hurricanes to watch practice and hopefully come away with a better understanding of how their coaching staff taught the vertical passing game. Obviously, Miami did lots of things on the football field very well. What Mumme and Leach were most impressed by was the ability of the Hurricanes' wide receivers to make catching balls thrown over their shoulders look routine and consistently complete the deep ball.

Once they arrived on campus and began to make their way to Miami's practice field, Mumme found himself feeling underwhelmed by the quality of the team's facilities. Mumme came from Texas where high schools routinely spent millions of dollars on football stadiums and provided their teams with weight rooms and practice fields to match that investment. Miami had just won its fourth national championship in nine years. The Hurricanes were the most talked about team in college football and most of their games were televised nationally. Money had to be rolling in from boosters, television contracts, and ticket sales, yet their workout facilities and practice field didn't look much better than the ones that the Tigers used back in Mount Pleasant. Mumme came to Miami expecting to find college football's Roman Empire of facilities, but in reality he had actually stumbled on a smoldering Pompeii.

Yet, somehow Miami found a way to go 84–13 over the past nine seasons against the best competition in the country in the process of winning four national championships. To Mumme, the message was clear: facilities don't matter. They're not nearly as important as the system a coach runs or the players found in that system. With that, Mumme was done complaining about the facilities at Iowa Wesleyan.

When practice ended, Leach and Mumme hung around hoping to speak with one of Miami's assistant coaches about what they had just seen. After loitering on the sidelines long enough, they managed to follow the herd into the coaches' locker room to catch up with head coach Dennis Erickson. Erickson emerged from the coaches' locker room freshly showered, wearing nothing but his boxer shorts and greeted the gridiron pilgrims. Erickson asked his visitors what they were interested in learning and Mumme explained that they were hoping to hear more about Miami's vertical passing game, particularly the techniques the Hurricanes' coaching staff taught that made their receivers so proficient at catching the deep ball. Miami's coach proved to be more focused on teaching than he was on dressing, and he marched right over to the chalkboard to begin a lecture about Miami's vertical passing game. The sermon went on for nearly an hour. In that time, Mumme peppered Erickson with questions on any concepts he wanted to hear more about while Leach spent the session frantically transcribing all of the important bits of insight that he could.

When their hour with Erickson was up Mumme and Leach had learned a lot about how to coach the deep ball. Perhaps the most important takeaway dealt

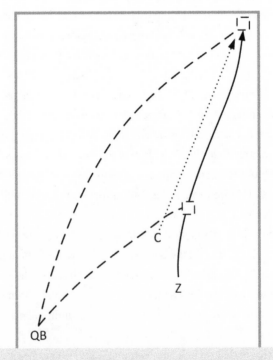

This was the path we had our receivers take on deep balls at Iowa Wesleyan before meeting with Dennis Erickson. Notice how the receiver's path drifts toward the sideline in an effort to create separation from the defensive back.

with where to send receivers once they beat a defensive back on a deep route. At the time, most coaches were teaching their receivers to fade their route toward the sideline once they beat the man covering them. Popular wisdom had it that running to the outside put more distance between the receiver and defensive back, leaving the receiver wide open. It was true that running away from defensive backs created greater separation, but it also left the defensive back in the line of the throw, providing them with a better opportunity to recover and make a play on the ball, especially if it was underthrown.

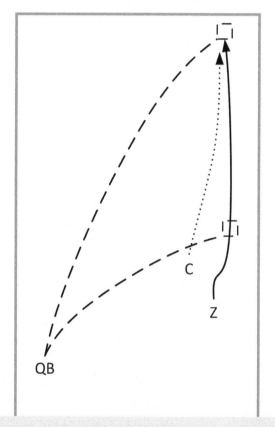

After our meeting with Dennis Erickson we taught our receivers to "stack" the defensive back covering them. If our receivers had a defensive back beat on a deep route, we would have them step in front of the defender to get a better position on the ball. Once a receiver stacks a defensive back, you've got the defense right where you want them. The only thing that the best defender can do on a well-thrown ball at this point is commit pass interference and hope it doesn't draw a flag.

Erickson had his receivers do just the opposite. When Miami's receivers beat the defender covering them deep, they were coached to reroute to the middle of the field to take the defensive back's spot on the inside. Sending the receiver to the inside cut off the defensive back's route to the ball, reducing their ability to make a play, and puts the receiver in control. For Mumme and Leach the change in direction was a major revelation. "We really didn't know how to throw the deep ball until then," explained Mumme.

After leaving Coral Gables, they continued to head south to meet with a talented kicker out of Key West High School named Steve Leonard. Mumme was hoping to see how well Leonard could kick in person, but the school's football field became the baseball field in the spring, and the goalposts had been taken down. Never at a loss for ideas, Mumme set up the football on a tee in front of the pitcher's mound and told Leonard to boot it over the backstop, which he did with ease. Mumme set up another football two yards in front of the previous spot and told Leonard, "Do it again." The kicker sent the ball flying over the backstop again with room to spare, so Mumme placed another football on a tee two yards in front of the previous spot and asked Leonard to replicate the previous results. Leonard responded with another towering kick that cleared the backstop easily.

So it went, with Mumme moving the ball forward in two yard increments and Leonard continuing to drill footballs well over the backstop. The idea was to make sure that Leonard was capable of getting enough lift on the ball to fly over the outstretched hands of defenders attempting to block the kick. By the time Leonard kicked a football over the backstop from home plate, Mumme figured it was time to offer the kicker a spot on the Tigers' roster. "How would you like to come to Iowa Wesleyan?" he asked.

Leonard was relieved. "Boy, I'd sure love to get off this rock," he said. Mumme was baffled by Leonard's longing to leave Key West for southeast Iowa but kept his thoughts to himself.

Later that night, Leach and Mumme convened at Captain Tony's Saloon to recap the day's events and dive head first into the Key West experience. Captain Tony's was owned by an old salt named Tony Tarracino, a Prohibition-era bootlegger, gambler, and storyteller from New Jersey who fled to Key West in 1948 after being beaten and left for dead in a Newark dump by the mafia. By the time Mumme and Leach were bellying up at his saloon, Tarracino was a fixture on the island and coming off his two-year tenure as mayor of Key West. He won election on the support of Jimmy Buffett, who wrote "Last Mango in Paris" about

Tarracino, and his intention to "limit Key West's growth and to keep its reputation as a refuge for eccentrics and renegades who found their way to the southernmost point of the continental United States." Clearly, Mumme and Leach had come to the right place.

The two sat at the bar for hours, firing down drinks, and talking about everything under the warm Key West sun until Mumme, exhausted from Cuban coffee-induced sleep deprivation and football road-tripping, called it quits. He headed back to the hotel, leaving Leach behind to enjoy the nightlife at Captain Tony's alone.

Mumme wound up regretting his decision the following afternoon when he caught up with Leach. "You missed it," Leach began as Mumme immediately began to cringe at the previous evening's decision to turn in early. Shortly after Mumme left, Tarracino pulled up a barstool next to Leach and proceeded to share the story behind "Last Mango in Paris." There were magnificent tales about marrying fashion models, working on Wall Street, and leading smugglers on a wild goose chase around the globe. It was an evening straight out of a Jimmy Buffett song, and Mumme couldn't believe that he missed it. Instead, he got to hear the story secondhand as he and Leach drove north to Orlando for their flight back to Chicago.

Along the way, they talked about the players that they'd recruited on their trip as well as the changes to the offense that they planned to implement once they returned to Mount Pleasant. Between the mixture of players they had on their hands and the schematic upgrades, Mumme and Leach agreed that they had a chance to be pretty darn good in 1991. And they thought that a successful season may even earn them an opportunity to take another step forward on the coaching ladder and deliver them to a school that could afford to pay the entire coaching staff a livable wage. Mumme thought about where he might like their next destination to be and asked Leach, "What about The Citadel? We've always liked Charleston. That might be a fun place to work."

It didn't take Leach long to shoot down the idea. "Nah," he said as he shook his head, casually dismissing the notion of working at the Military College of South Carolina. "I want to play pirate if I have to play something."

Captain Tony would have been proud.

9

FOOTBALL FAMILY

Mike Fanoga first caught Mumme's eye when he was a sophomore linebacker at Snow Community College in Ephraim, Utah, in 1984. The native from American Samoa was in the process of completing his junior college eligibility and hoping to catch on at a four-year school to earn his bachelor's degree and continue his football career. Mumme, then the offensive coordinator at the University of Texas at El Paso, was in Utah on a recruiting trip to see Snow's quarterback when he kept on hearing "Fanoga on the tackle" over the loudspeaker while Snow's defense was on the field. Mumme was impressed with what he saw from the feisty linebacker. Fanoga finished the game with nearly twenty tackles and an opportunity to finish his degree and play football in El Paso.

In Fanoga's first season at El Paso he proved himself to be a dogged competitor and a tough, rugged player. About halfway through the 1985 season, Mumme was in the locker room when he overheard a member of the training staff explaining to the linebackers coach that Fanoga had been diagnosed with a torn anterior cruciate ligament (ACL) and would have to be sidelined for the rest of the season. It was disappointing for Mumme to hear that a player he had recruited suffered such a serious injury, but risks like that were part of the game. With proper treatment and some luck, he'd see Fanoga on the field next season. Needless to say, Mumme was shocked when he made his way to the practice field and found Fanoga already there, stretching in full pads and suited up for practice.

The 1985 season would be the pair's only season together in El Paso. The coaching staff that Mumme was a part of was fired after the season, and Fanoga finished his collegiate eligibility under a new coaching regime. Following his senior season, Fanoga joined the coaching staff as a graduate assistant. After spending two more years at his alma mater earning his master's degree in physical education, he moved on to the University of West Alabama where he coached for two more seasons before running into Mumme at the American Football Coaches Association Convention in San Francisco in January 1990. Fanoga took the opportunity to thank Mumme for giving him the opportunity to play college football and brought his former coach up to speed on his experiences on the sidelines over the past four seasons. Mumme took the opportunity to extend another invitation to his former recruit, this time to join him on the sidelines at Iowa Wesleyan as an assistant coach, which Fanoga gladly accepted.

Fanoga's hiring immediately tapped Iowa Wesleyan's football program into a pipeline of Polynesian talent from all over the United States. Although he had not grown up in American Samoa himself, Fanoga's family had strong connections to the island and its tightly knit community. While the families of the recruits he pursued may not have known Fanoga personally, odds were that they or someone in their family knew the name Fanoga and some members of his extended family. As a result, Fanoga didn't have any trouble finding common ground with Polynesian players or credibility with their families. For the families, the name Fanoga was trustworthy, a convenient recruiting edge that Fanoga took extremely seriously. For Fanoga, his name didn't simply carry credibility, it carried the accountability to live up to each and every promise that he made while he was on the recruiting trail.

When Fanoga walked into a home to offer a recruit the opportunity to continue their football career, he would offer their family reassurance that their son would have a chance to play football, get their degree, and be safe at a school that was far away from home in most cases. It wasn't just a recruiting pitch, it was a promise. If Fanoga didn't follow through and those recruits didn't come home with a degree in four years, he knew it would put a black mark on his family name as well as the young man he'd recruited and failed to send home with a degree. "It would make me look bad, it would make him look bad, and then we'd both be failures," says Fanoga of the pressure he felt, and continues to feel, to ensure the success of his recruits.

When Polynesian players came to Mount Pleasant to play for Iowa Wesleyan, Fanoga quickly established himself as their "football father." It wasn't unusual for

Fanoga and his wife Soana to gather the players at their home for a good home-cooked meal and an opportunity to connect on a personal level outside of football. It's what parents do after all.

Parents also relentlessly pester their children about their homework and ensure that they make it to school on time every day. Fanoga aggressively took on this role as well. He was his most vigilant when it came to the academic pursuits of his adopted football sons. During the winter of 1991, it was normal to see Fanoga, sporting shorts and work boots marching through a fresh blanket of snow between the academic buildings on Iowa Wesleyan's campus. He was followed closely by a procession of colossal Polynesians bundled up like Ralphie, Randy, Flick, and Schwartz, who were being led to class by their football coach.

The bonds forged among Fanoga's Polynesian recruits constituted a strong part of the nucleus of what would prove to be a remarkably tight-knit team going into the 1991 season. Although it might seem difficult to spot similarities between country boys from central Texas, city kids from Chicago, and a gregarious pack of Samoans, the bottom line is that they were all just kids playing football a thousand miles away from home. Once they established that common ground, their differences helped to keep life interesting in a tiny town that seemed pretty dead outside of a handful of weekends at Mapleleaf Field each fall. The ones who actually came from Iowa were just happy to have the type of characters around who brought something other than the status quo.

Mount Pleasant and Iowa Wesleyan's roster was an ideal marriage of personalities and setting that created an exceptional camaraderie among the team leading into the 1991 season. It's a good thing that they got along, too. Mumme made sure that the team spent plenty of time together, regardless of the time of year.

During the previous offseason, Mumme had the team spend their Tuesday nights in an old gym on Iowa Wesleyan's campus perfecting the shotgun snap and other wrinkles he was planning to implement during the 1990 season. Midnight Maneuvers returned in the 1991 offseason, this time to work on some of the finer points of the no-huddle offense.

Mumme's experience with the no-huddle offense was limited to a game during his time at El Paso back in 1982. The Miners were facing off against a physically superior opponent in Arizona State, so Mumme had the offense start the game by operating out of the no-huddle in an effort to throw the Sun Devils defense off balance. It worked remarkably well, and the Miners had little trouble moving the ball during their first two drives and managed to put up six points in the process.

The tactic also pissed off the undefeated Pac-10 team something awful, and the Sun Devils went on to pummel the Miners with 37 unanswered points after those first two drives. However, the early success of the no-huddle during that game was enough to get Mumme thinking that it would provide just the edge that the Tigers would need for the 1991 season. The insight and practice methods that Don Matthews shared with Mumme during the Florida pilgrimage earlier that winter proved to be crucial. Matthews' two-minute practice drill that Mumme repackaged into Iowa Wesleyan's bandit drill was the method that he would use to bring his players up to speed on the finer points of the no-huddle before game day.

Because of Iowa Wesleyan's expulsion from the Illini-Badger-Hawkeye Conference, the Tigers were going to move up to compete as an NAIA Division I Independent. The schedule included contests with a number of NCAA Division II opponents as well as substantially improved competition at their own level thanks to the team's competitive step forward. Mumme's team needed to evolve if they wanted to maintain their winning ways against that type of opposition, a lesson that the team had learned all too well from the combined 95–6 drubbings that they suffered at the hands of Portland State and Morningside to start the previous season. Those losses served as motivation for the players throughout the offseason. The Tigers were acutely aware of the level of play they would have to maintain throughout the season if they wanted to be competitive and they were enthusiastic about improving every day throughout the offseason.

Wide receivers Marcus Washington and Bruce Carter kept the team motivated throughout Midnight Maneuvers and spring practice with their work ethic and vocal leadership. Their words and their actions issued a challenge to the other members of the team each and every day to match their effort. Meanwhile, Dustin Dewald's quiet, confident leadership kept the team focused on the task at hand, even if he wasn't crazy about some of the new wrinkles to Mumme's offense.

These days, there's no shortage of offenses that have their quarterback call the plays at the line of scrimmage without huddling. During the winter of 1991, the list of quarterbacks with in-game experience running the no-huddle began with Boomer Esiason of the Cincinnati Bengals and ended with the University of Houston's David Klingler. Outside of those two, there weren't a whole lot of names in between. The no-huddle was a fairly revolutionary concept at the time, and Dewald was having a difficult time getting a handle on the play-calling aspect of things, particularly choosing a play at the line of scrimmage after he'd called one only fifteen seconds ago. It's one thing to have a strong handle on an offense, it's quite another to consistently choose the best play three or four times every minute while taking into account things like score, time remaining, field position, down, distance, offensive personnel, defensive personnel, coverage, blitzes, and so on. And it wasn't as if Dewald didn't already have enough on his mind.

Iowa Wesleyan's rising senior quarterback wasn't exactly in the middle of what could be considered a prototypical college experience. Off the field, Dewald's existence in Mount Pleasant didn't share much in common with that of his teammates. He was also a husband to his wife Tiffany, and his everyday life reflected that title much more so than student–athlete.

After Dewald's first year in Mount Pleasant, he bought a 650-square foot, one-bedroom, one-bathroom house in town that he immediately began working on. Dewald's father and grandfather were homebuilders in Texas, and they were generous in sharing whatever knowledge and materials they could spare in Dustin's home improvement efforts.

By the time Dewald finished his first season at Iowa Wesleyan, his family had gotten quite familiar with the thousand-mile trip between Copperas Cove and Mount Pleasant. The Friday afternoon of every home game, the Dewald family would pack up the car and begin driving to Iowa. They would drive through the night, arriving in town on Saturday morning with enough time to say a quick hello to Dustin before he started pregame warm-ups and set up a tailgate in the parking lot at Mapleleaf Field. After the game, the Dewalds would stick around for Saturday night and then hop in the car early Sunday afternoon to make the long journey back home to Texas. When Dustin and Tiffany bought their house, his parents started bringing materials with them to Iowa and added home improvement to the list of weekend activities.

The Dewald family's efforts weren't limited to elementary activities like painting, carpeting, and tiling. No, they were straight up remodeling, adding a garage, two bedrooms, and a bathroom to the once tiny house. When Dustin graduated from Iowa Wesleyan in December 1991, only two years after buying the home, it had grown to 1,600 square feet thanks to the steady flow of materials and expertise coming from Texas, not to mention his and Tiffany's hard work throughout the week and during the offseason when his family couldn't be on hand to assist with the home improvement efforts.

While working on the house kept the Dewalds plenty busy, it certainly wasn't going to pay the mortgage. Subsequently, Dustin and Tiffany held a variety of jobs during their time in Mount Pleasant to make ends meet. In addition to her studies at Iowa Wesleyan, Tiffany worked in the football offices on campus as Mumme's secretary and as a cashier at a grocery store in town. Meanwhile, Dewald worked as a grill cook at a restaurant in a local truck stop until he was able to find work as a bartender at an Irish bar near town. The patrons weren't exactly generous, and by Dewald's calculation he made more money hustling pool when the bar was slow than he did in gratuities from customers. Even so, it beat sweating bullets over a grease fire in a poorly ventilated kitchen for hours at a time, so he had a smile on his face most nights as he wiped down the bar after last call.

When Dewald and Tiffany returned to campus for the 1991 spring semester, they knew it would be the last that they would get to spend together in Mount Pleasant. Tiffany was set to graduate from Iowa Wesleyan in May, and after receiving her diploma she planned to return home to Copperas Cove to begin her teaching career, leaving Dewald behind to complete his degree and his collegiate eligibility. Spending almost half a year a thousand miles apart certainly wasn't an ideal situation, but it was not as if they were going to be spending that time alone. Tiffany returned to her family and friends back in Texas while Dewald would spend the year surrounded by his adopted football family in Iowa.

Robert Draper, a student assistant who was helping Leach coach the offensive line, wound up moving in with Dewald after Tiffany graduated. The two were old friends and teammates who had played together at Copperas Cove for Mumme before following him to Iowa Wesleyan. Draper had completed his playing eligibility after the 1990 season, but he was sticking around Mount Pleasant to finish up his degree and get some coaching experience under his belt. As close as the pair had been before and during their time in Mount Pleasant, Draper didn't exactly fill the void left by Tiffany's absence. Nonetheless, it was helpful to have someone around to lend a helping hand with the continued renovations to Chateau Dewald and provide some company. In the latter respect, Draper was not alone.

During their time at Iowa Wesleyan, Dewald and Draper had seen a number of players come and go. Some, like Mike Jefferson, left Mount Pleasant on their own accord in a blaze of glory and striptease bravado. Others left town in a less deliberate and more inconspicuous fashion, such as phone card thief Jimmy Korn. The players who managed to last throughout their tenure and make it to camp in 1991 were high-character guys who were fully invested in the team that they had essentially started. The same could be said for the overwhelming majority of the guys who were brought to campus after that first recruiting season, when the coaches weren't forced to frantically gather players like little kids scooping up scattered candy from a busted piñata.

Thanks to the shared experiences, goals, and work ethic, Dewald and his receiving corps had developed a strong chemistry with one another as they were heading into the 1991 season. Veteran wide receivers Marcus Washington, Bruce Cater, and Dana Holgorsen were all talented, savvy players that had plenty of in-game experience catching passes from Dewald, not to mention the countless repetitions on the practice field. After logging hundreds of hours watching film together, all three knew how to read defenses, understood how to adjust their routes in response to different defensive schemes, and Dewald knew exactly where on the field he could find them.

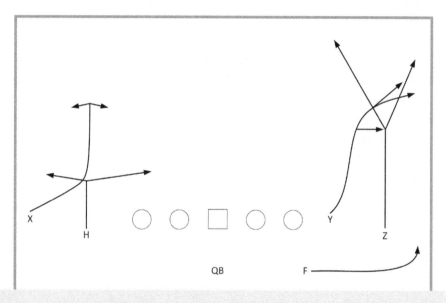

The great thing about having experienced receivers in our offense is that they can react to any defensive coverage. Dana Holgorsen (Z), Bruce Carter (H), and Marcus Washington (Y) made the sail route unstoppable.

Dewald also found himself in tune with his offensive line during preseason workouts. Virtually the entire offensive line had been protecting Dewald since his first season at Iowa Wesleyan. The only newcomer to the line was Bill Bedenbaugh who was taking the vacancy left by former center and new strength coach John Coneset. He got with the program quickly. Each player on the offensive line understood what the offense was trying to accomplish on each snap, picked up blitzes well, and knew how much time their quarterback needed to get rid of the ball, which wasn't a whole lot. One of the things Dewald did best was quickly recognize the vulnerabilities that certain blitz packages created in the defense and immediately deliver the ball exactly where the defense had left itself exposed. The strength and experience of the offensive unit made Dewald's early struggles with the play-calling aspect of running the no-huddle much more manageable than it would have been otherwise.

Also helping matters was Mumme's decision to significantly trim the playbook over the offseason. Instead of having to select a play from the entire playbook, Dewald was given a half dozen plays to run from a variety of formations when the Tigers' offense was operating out of the no-huddle. The simplified version of Iowa Wesleyan's offense alleviated the mental stress of running through a few dozen plays in the matter of seconds between snaps. With the pared down playbook, Dewald didn't have to consider dozens of play calls in his head as he hustled to the line of scrimmage to bark out the next play to his teammates. After a rocky spring practice, Dewald began confidently running the no-huddle and calling plays with the same amount of ease he'd run the offense for the previous two seasons when preseason camp rolled around in August.

10

BEGINNING OF THE END

I n his 1883 historical memoir *Life on the Mississippi*, Mark Twain observed, "All the Upper Mississippi region has these extraordinary sunsets as a familiar spectacle. It is the true Sunset Land: I am sure no other country can show so good a right to the name." It's a sentiment that is not lost on anyone who's spent any amount of time in Mount Pleasant. For farmers across the Hawkeye State, the sun slowly easing its way toward the horizon signals a close to the workday and brings with it reprieve from hot summer days on the plains. Anyone who cares to set their gaze westward as the afternoon creeps into the evening finds a progressive work of art becoming ever more brilliant with each fleeting moment. It's a time to pause, reflect, and give thanks for another homespun day along the Mississippi.

However, on August 31, 1991, much of Mount Pleasant allowed the Iowa sun to set in relative anonymity because their collective gaze was set on Mapleleaf Field for Iowa Wesleyan's season opener. For the second consecutive season, the expectations surrounding Mumme's Tigers were through the roof. All-American quarterback Dustin Dewald was leading a veteran offensive unit into the school's first season competing at the NAIA Division I level. The defense had improved significantly under Charlie Moot's direction over the course of the previous season and the program was beginning to attract considerably more local talent. All indications suggested that a powerhouse was beginning to come into its own in southeast Iowa.

Also for the second consecutive season, Iowa Wesleyan's schedule began with a veritable buzz saw of talented opponents that competed at the NCAA Division II level. On this night, Northeast Missouri State University awaited Mumme's squad in the visitors' locker room. The Bulldogs came into the game ranked tenth in the nation in the preseason polls coming off a season in which they had finished sixth in the nation in total offense while holding five opponents to seven points or less defensively. Their departed quarterback was a finalist for the Harlon Hill Trophy, NCAA Division II's version of the Heisman Trophy. He was replaced by a highly touted six-foot, five-inch, 235-pound transfer from the University of Missouri. The Bulldogs surrounded their new quarterback with an experienced core of skill position players, many of whom were candidates for All-American accolades.

Meanwhile, in the home locker room at Mapleleaf Field, Mumme paced and mentally prepared himself for a monumental sixty minutes of football. This was a huge game. The stadium was packed because fans of both schools eagerly bought whatever tickets were available to see the first game pitting the Tigers against the Bulldogs since the Truman administration. To the inexperienced observer, Iowa Wesleyan and Northeast Missouri would seem to be natural rivals. Kirksville and Mount Pleasant were both farming towns separated by only ninety miles in a sparsely populated region of the country. Each community placed a strong value on education, with one boasting a private college whereas the other boasted a public institution. Only three years ago the idea of the two schools competing against one another on the gridiron would have been completely absurd and a horribly embarrassing endeavor for Iowa Wesleyan. In terms of level of competition and funding, a wide competitive gap still remained between the two programs, but Mumme's prolific offense led Tiger fans to believe that their team belonged on the same field as the Bulldogs.

As Mumme oversaw pregame warm-ups, he found nary an empty seat in Mapleleaf Field's bleachers, save a section of about two dozen seats reserved for Iowa Wesleyan's faculty and staff. As he roamed the field, he watched cheerleaders sprinting across the sidelines carrying Iowa Wesleyan flags to the cheers of an already frenzied crowd. The scene was a far cry from a school that refused to charge admission just two years before and another indication that the football program had arrived.

Now that the team was back in the locker room, there was nothing to do but wait until it was time to return to the field for the coin flip and opening kickoff. Outside of the locker room, Mumme had paid plenty of lip service to his highly regarded opponents, commenting to one local reporter before the game, "We know too much about them, and they are scaring us to death. Their quarterback should be starting for the University of Missouri. They are just a great football team." When his commentary wasn't being made available for print, Mumme thought and said otherwise. In his own locker room, he was surrounded by a prolific and battle-tested team of his own that was minutes away from unleashing sixty minutes of no-huddle offense, a look that their opponents, not to mention much of the Midwest, had never seen before.

Mumme took his place in front of his team and looked at dozens of familiar and determined faces staring right back at him. He wasted no time in telling them exactly what he thought their chances were that night against Northeast Missouri State. "Guys," he began, "we're gonna go out there and kick their ass." He took a moment to let the statement sink in, to make sure his team knew that he meant it and that they believed it themselves before he went on. "And the reason is because we're a better team." It was all that needed to be said. Mumme turned and made his way for the locker room exit, followed by dozens of coaches and players who were hell-bent on proving him right.

The game's early goings saw Iowa Wesleyan trade punches with a fierce opponent. Northeast Missouri started the scoring with a 24-yard field goal after their opening drive stalled at the 7-yard line. The Tigers responded quickly as Dewald delivered a 33-yard touchdown pass to Bruce Carter on the ensuing possession for a 7–3 advantage. The lead lasted until Iowa Wesleyan's next possession when their drive stalled near midfield and were forced to march out their punt team. Northeast Missouri's punt coverage team burst through the Tigers' protection, blocked the punt, recovered the ball, and promptly ran it into the end zone to claim a 10–7 edge. From there, the rest of the first half belonged to the Bulldogs.

Northeast Missouri's talented offensive unit went on to throw for two more touchdowns in the second quarter. Meanwhile, their defense allowed Iowa Wesleyan's new look no-huddle offense to move the ball, but managed to keep them off the scoreboard for the rest of the half. The Bulldogs headed into the locker room at halftime holding a commanding 24–7 lead over the Tigers.

Mumme began what he thought would be a long walk to the locker room wondering what exactly he had been thinking when he agreed to bring the Bulldogs to Mount Pleasant for his team's season opener. He just as easily could have taken his team on the road to get lit up by a nationally ranked NCAA Division II squad and earned a hefty payday in the process. Instead he'd brought one to Mapleleaf Field so that a home crowd could have front row seats for a shellacking instead of reading about it in the newspaper the next morning. Before Mumme could get lost in the flashbacks he was having to the Morningside and Portland State games that the Tigers lost by a combined 95–6 to start the previous season, he had two interactions that completely changed his outlook on a fresh season that had only just begun.

The first came as he walked past offensive tackle Shawn Martin. Martin was one of the more unassuming guys on the team and despite the fact that he was a fine football player, he didn't register high in the self-confidence department. However, as Mumme walked by Martin the two locked eyes. Very matter-of-factly, Martin spit out, "Don't worry, coach, we're going to win this game." Taken back by the unexpected show of confidence, Mumme merely nodded his head and continued on his path toward the locker room.

Ten yards later Mumme crossed paths with Dewald, who promptly offered his frank assessment of the second-half's prospects. "Coach, you don't need to say anything at halftime," his quarterback began, "we're gonna kick their ass." Dewald's comment was a bit more in character, but Mumme was still amused by his players' buoyancy as he continued to shuffle his way toward the locker room and wondered what had gotten into his players that left them so self-assured. As he reflected on the first half on a deeper level, Mumme began to share his players' confidence. Despite their inability to score after their first possession, the Tigers' offense wasn't having trouble moving the ball. The pace of the game created by the no-huddle was wearing on Northeast Missouri's players, and it was beginning to show. As time dwindled in the first half, Iowa Wesleyan's players couldn't ignore the fatigue they saw in the players lining up across from them and recognized that their opponents were vulnerable. The offense knew that they were going to score plenty in the second half, and if the defense could manage to get some stops and keep the Bulldogs off the scoreboard, they knew that they would have a chance.

The second half started with Iowa Wesleyan's defense holding up its end of the bargain and forcing a Northeast Missouri punt. Once again, the Tigers' offense managed to move the ball some before their drive stalled around midfield. However, when the Tigers lined up to punt, they found themselves lined up against twelve Bulldogs. The referee flagged Northeast Missouri for too many men on the field, giving the Tigers five yards, a first down, and the opening that they needed to begin to take control of the game.

On the first play from scrimmage after the penalty, Dewald found Marcus Washington for a 30-yard completion, bringing the offense to the 9-yard line. Chann Chavis caught a 9-yard touchdown pass on the next play, bringing the score to 24–13 after a botched extra point. For the rest of the third quarter neither offense could get much going and Iowa Wesleyan entered the game's final 15 minutes in an 11-point hole.

In the fourth quarter, with the Bulldog defense sucking wind from keeping up with Iowa Wesleyan's unrelenting no-huddle offense for three quarters, the Tigers really began to light up the scoreboard. Dewald began the game's final period by capping a drive with a 2-yard touchdown pass to Carter. A successful two-point conversion brought the score to 24–21. Moot's defensive unit continued their stingy second-half play on Northeast Missouri's ensuing possession and returned the ball to Dewald's capable hands with the three-point margin intact. Again, they had little trouble moving the ball through the Bulldog defense all the way to the eight yard-line before Dewald found Carter in the end zone for the wide receiver's second touchdown on the evening and a 28–24 Iowa Wesleyan lead with 6 minutes and 48 seconds remaining. Three minutes later, Marcus Washington reeled in a 51-yard touchdown pass from Dewald, extending the lead to 34–24, which turned out to be too much for mighty Northeast Missouri to overcome.

The Bulldogs scored another touchdown before the game's final whistle, but it mattered little to a team that had just posted the biggest win in school history. For a group of guys that had already achieved so much in Mount Pleasant, the win represented a huge accomplishment, perhaps their biggest to date. After suffering two lopsided losses to start the previous season against similar competition, the win signified just how much the team had improved in only a year's time. The win was also a message to the rest of the country, and confirmation for themselves, that Iowa Wesleyan was ready to compete for a national championship.

However, in a pre-Internet United States, the rest of the country was slow to get the message. The Tigers remained unranked in the next week's NAIA Division I poll as they prepared for a matchup with lowly University of Missouri–Rolla who had snapped a 19-game losing streak in their season opener. Iowa Wesleyan escaped that game with a 21–17 victory thanks to a rugged defensive effort led by safety Rodger Bowers. Bowers preserved the victory by intercepting a pass in the end zone with ten minutes left in the fourth quarter before forcing a fumble at the goal line with four minutes left in the game. "I think our defense won the game," said Mumme afterward. Despite a lackluster performance against Missouri–Rolla, pollsters ranked Iowa Wesleyan number 20 in the nation on the strength of their 2–0 start.

A week later, Iowa Wesleyan and its emerging defense found itself in another scrappy game, this time a 13–7 win over Midwestern State University in Wichita Falls, Texas. The win catapulted the Tigers to 3–0 and number 12 in the next week's NAIA Division I poll heading into a matchup with eighteenth-ranked Harding College at Burlington's Bracewell Stadium, the site of the previous two Steamboat Bowls.

It's worth noting that Mumme's wife June had played a key role in bringing her husband's high-flying offense back to Burlington for a regular season showdown. June had graduated from Iowa Wesleyan the previous May with a 3.6 GPA and a degree in business administration that she was eager to put to work. While being married to the school's head football coach had its advantages, it also came with some drawbacks, one of which being the suspicion of prospective employers' that she and her family might not be in town for long. Consequently, she had trouble finding work in Mount Pleasant.

Naturally, her husband saw her trouble finding a job as an opportunity to create one for her that would contribute to his efforts with the football program. Mumme went to Iowa Wesleyan booster John Wright to suggest that the booster club create a position for June as a fundraiser and marketing director. She had done similar work promoting fundraising events back in Copperas Cove and proved herself quite capable of rallying community support. The booster club signed off on the arrangement, compensating her with 10 percent of the money she raised.

June made the rounds at local businesses to drum up support for the Tigers in the form of season ticket sales, corporate sponsorships, and other advertising. She sold sponsorships for each of the football team's home games for $1,000 apiece and suggested moving the Harding game to Burlington to capitalize on the additional seating available at Bracewell Stadium. Heading into the season it seemed like a good bet that the matchup would generate plenty of local excitement. Iowa Wesleyan's team figured to be even better than they were during the first two seasons of Mumme's tenure and Harding was an NAIA powerhouse. Mumme liked the idea, and when game day arrived the stands at Bracewell Stadium were packed to see Iowa Wesleyan take on Harding.

The school from Little Rock, Arkansas finished the previous season ranked fifteenth in the nation among NAIA Division I schools but was off to a rocky start in the 1991 campaign. They came into the game with a 1–2 record, having dropped its season opener to NCAA I-AA Samford University before losing on the final play to highly rated Northeastern State University two weeks later. Despite the losing record, the Bisons boasted one of the best pass defenses in the nation, giving up only seventy-eight yards through the air per game.

Harding figured to be a formidable opponent even if Iowa Wesleyan had been coming into the game with a clean bill of health. The Tigers' leading receiver Carter was sidelined for the game with a sprained ankle that he suffered the previous week. Considering his opponent and the injury report, popular wisdom might suggest that if there was ever a situation for Mumme to give his rushing attack a more prominent role in the game plan, this was it. However, it was more likely that Mumme was going to heed the wisdom of Thomas Jonathan "Stonewall" Jackson who said, "Never take counsel of your fears." The Tigers had Dewald and a capable stable of wide receivers, even with Carter out of the lineup. Mumme knew what his team did best, and that was air it out. On that chilly September evening at Bracewell Stadium, he had Dewald air it out more than any collegiate quarterback ever had.

The Harding game was a shootout. Iowa Wesleyan began the scoring when Dewald found Carter's replacement, freshman wide receiver Chris Oepping in the end zone halfway through the first quarter. Harding responded, and so it went throughout the rest of the evening as each team fought to maintain its advantage with little success. The lead changed hands four times in the second half and the outcome wasn't decided until the Bisons' punt block team got a hand on Bill Link's punt late in the fourth quarter with Iowa Wesleyan clinging to a 31–28 lead. The blocked punt brought Harding's offense back onto the field at the Tigers' 15-yard line. Three plays later their quarterback snuck the ball into the end zone from 1 yard out for a 35–31 victory.

Despite the loss, it had been a record-breaking evening for Dewald. On that night he threw for 444 yards on 61 completions in 86 attempts. The completions and attempts were both good for national collegiate records at any level. However, the records came at a price.

With ten seconds left in the first half, Iowa Wesleyan's defense forced a turnover near midfield. Wanting to take advantage of the opportunity, Mumme told Dewald to run Big Ben, a Hail Mary–type play where three receivers lined up on one side of the formation and ran to the end zone to wait for a bomb from the quarterback. Dewald, never a big fan of the play in the first place, didn't think Big Ben was a good call for the situation, so he looked back at Mumme and said,

"No." Mumme's eyes got wide and he shouted back that Dewald had better run what he called, to which his quarterback begrudgingly agreed.

On the ensuing play Dewald threw an interception to a Harding defensive back. After the defensive back slipped out of attempted tackles by Iowa Wesleyan receivers, the speedy defenseman weaved through a pack of offensive linemen lumbering down the field after him. Dewald, the Tigers' last line of defense, managed to track down Harding's defensive back in the open field and proceeded to bury his right shoulder into the ball carrier's torso and bring him to the ground as time expired. As he made the tackle, Dewald felt his right shoulder give and began to feel a sharp, nagging pain in his shoulder as he got to his feet. As the team jogged off the field into the locker room Dewald yelled at Mumme, "Good goddamn call!" Those words were the only indication that Dewald would give that he'd been hurt, despite the incessant pain in his shoulder for the rest of the game. He woke up the next morning in excruciating pain, unable to move his throwing arm and decided it was about time to head to the training room to find out what was wrong.

On Monday, Mumme joined his quarterback in the training room before practice. Nancy Turner, Iowa Wesleyan's trainer ran some tests on the injured shoulder and diagnosed Dewald with a partially torn rotator cuff. Turner presented Dewald with two options for how to proceed with the injury, neither of which seemed desirable. First, he could have season-ending surgery on the shoulder to repair the torn rotator cuff. As a senior, season-ending surgery meant that Dewald would never play football again. That option was quickly disregarded.

The second option Turner presented was to postpone surgery until the end of the season and allow Dewald to play through the torn rotator cuff by limiting the strain he put on the shoulder. At the most, he would be able to throw one day a week, meaning that Dewald would be unable to practice between games, a tough situation considering he directed an offense that required him to throw the ball forty to fifty times a game and relied on timing and chemistry among its skill position players. Even so, the decision was a "no-brainer" for Dewald. He would play so long as his shoulder allowed and get surgery at the end of the season.

From a player safety perspective, Mumme had his apprehensions about sending his quarterback onto the field for the rest of the season knowing that he had a torn rotator cuff. Nonetheless, he left the decision in Dewald's hands. Dewald was abundantly more mature than the average college football player, and he was well aware of the risks of playing with his injury. Either way, his football career was coming to a close and playing through the pain would at least give him seven more games under center.

From a player productivity and effectiveness standpoint, Mumme had no apprehension about Dewald finishing out the season before his surgery. "Dustin Dewald was the unequivocal leader of our offense," Mumme explained. The intangibles that Dewald brought to the table, particularly the respect of his teammates, which he had earned, and the chemistry that he had developed with the rest of the offense, trumped any concerns that Mumme may have had regarding his ability to make the throws. He would give Dewald the opportunity to retain his job with his performance on Saturdays. Frankly, he earned it.

One of the biggest challenges Mumme faced as a result of Dewald's injury was figuring out how to incorporate him into Iowa Wesleyan's practices throughout the week. Mumme's practices required every quarterback from the starter to the last on the depth chart to throw hundreds of balls. That option was now off the table. Keeping Dewald engaged in practices would be more about the mental aspects of playing the position rather than the physical.

When the offense lined up against the defensive scout team, Mumme had Dewald stand a couple yards behind backup quarterback John Robinson. When Robinson approached the line of scrimmage to survey the defense and set up behind the center, Dewald would stand a couple yards behind him and call a play for the offense to run based on the defensive look. Once Robinson received the snap and the play began to unfold, Dewald would go through his read progression and call out where to deliver the football. It turned out to be a surprisingly effective arrangement. Even with Dewald in sweatpants, he was logging plenty of mental reps throughout the week while giving his injured shoulder the rest it needed to be ready to go on Saturday. The overwhelming majority of the team supported Mumme's decision wholeheartedly.

Of course, not everybody was on board for the unorthodox arrangement. Moot took issue with Mumme's decision to play Dewald on Saturdays when he wouldn't be taking snaps at team workouts during the week. To Moot, a retired Marine, the issue was a matter of principle. He thought that continuing to start a player who didn't fully participate in practice undermined the team concept by eliminating the incentive for the other players to give their best effort between games. It was seemingly sound logic, but it ignored the basic fact that Dewald was courageously putting himself and his future at risk every Saturday and giving 100 percent of the effort in practice that his health would allow. It also didn't hurt that most of the team would have followed Dewald into the depths of hell so long as he had the ball in his hands, so Mumme ignored the protests of his defensive coordinator and went ahead with the plan to continue playing Dewald.

If Dewald's shoulder and Moot's flawed logic were the only bumps in the road Mumme would have to deal with, the rest of the season would have been a walk in the park.

11

"You've got to go away."

Mumme was standing on the practice field directing day two of the Dustin Dewald ghost-quarterbacking experiment as his future began taking a turn for the murky. Iowa Wesleyan's ranking had dropped three spots to number fifteen in the nation after the Harding loss and the team was preparing for Saturday's homecoming game against Baker University. Although Baker competed a division below Iowa Wesleyan, the NAIA Division II squad was a formidable opponent. The program was a perennial contender at the national level, having qualified for the national playoffs in seven of the past eight seasons and came into the game ranked ninth in the country among its peers in Division II. The looming showdown with Baker had Mumme's undivided attention at the moment, but after practice he was to head to the president's office at the request of Dr. Robert Prins who had called him earlier that afternoon. The timing of the impromptu meeting seemed a bit unusual, but the season was off to an exceptional start despite the Harding loss. It didn't even occur to Mumme that he might have something to worry about.

When Mumme arrived at the administration building at 3:30, he found Dr. Prins waiting for him on the first floor. He seemed to be the only person in the office. Unsure of what exactly was going on, Mumme asked, "What do you need?"

Prins took a deep breath and looked back at Mumme. "Well," he began before taking a moment to decide the best way to drop a bomb, "you've got to go away."

"Excuse me?" shuddered an incredulous Mumme. Four games into his third season, he'd won nearly twice as many games as the program had in the previous

115

four. The program had been completely rebuilt during his tenure and the team was beginning to reach heights that seemed impossible before he arrived on campus. Mumme wasn't even four weeks removed from the season-opening win over Northeast Missouri State, the biggest win in school history and here he was, essentially being told that he was fired.

Prins broke an uncomfortable silence between the two men by clarifying his previous statement, "As soon as the season's over, you've got to go away."

As the news began to sink in and Mumme began to compose himself, he thought for a moment and offered the most gentlemanly response he could come up with: "I always said that if you didn't like me I'd do that for you, so I will."

"It's not that I don't like you," responded Prins. "You're over budget."

The president's rationale left Mumme indignant. "I'm not," he said defiantly. Football-related expenses had certainly gone up in his three years at Iowa Wesleyan, so there was a grain of truth in the loaf of bread Prins had used to concoct the turd sandwich that Mumme was now being served. However, the fact remained revenue had also increased over the past three years as well. Sure, the team had flown to Oregon for the Portland State game the previous season, a rarity for NAIA schools, but Portland State had covered Iowa Wesleyan's travel expenses and paid the school another $10,000. "So it seems to me that isn't what this is about."

Without acknowledging Mumme's assertion, Prins went on, "We're going to pay you through the end of December, and then you and all of your coaches need to go away. There's been great improvement in the football program since you've gotten here, but at the end of the season, you need to go away."

Frustrated with Prins' refusal to elaborate on his claim of football being over budget and discuss the matter further, Mumme got up from his chair and began to walk out of the office. When he got to the door, a thought crossed his mind that made him turn back to the president's desk. Mumme asked, "What about that contract you gave me in January?"

"I guess your lawyer can call our lawyer," said Prins with a shrug. "One more thing: make sure to tell your staff that they're only getting paid through the end of December, but if they want the job they should come see me."

With that, Mumme began a long walk home. By any standards, the meeting had been exceptionally cold-blooded. It was made worse by the fact that Mumme's teams had been exceeding expectations on the football field ever since he took control of the program. He had taken a winless NAIA Division II football program with no players and insufficient facilities and built it into the fifteenth-ranked team in NAIA Division I in only three years' time. The community was taking a genuine interest in the team and local talent was enthusiastically coming to Iowa Wesleyan's campus for the opportunity to play for Mumme. A national championship actually seemed to be within the team's grasp. None of that mattered. Come December he was going to be looking for work again, and his family would be uprooted in the process.

Mumme's thoughts began to drift from contemplating why he was being fired to wondering how he was going to explain to June and the kids that the family would be moving again at the end of the year. To aid the thought process he made a detour to pick up a bottle of Jack Daniels to help him work up the nerve to approach the subject with his wife when he got home.

It was a difficult conversation. June kept trying to wrap her head around why her husband was being fired, figuring that he had to have done something wrong to get fired after all of the games his teams had won. She knew her husband had a strong personality that had the potential to rub people the wrong way. During Mumme's first coaching job at Moody High School fifteen years before, June had been a substitute teacher and occasionally checked her husband's mailbox in the teacher's room. She regularly found notes from the principal that simply had the words "See me" scrawled on a piece of paper.

Mumme continued to assure her that he had not done anything wrong, but still all that she could think to say was "Why?" She believed her husband, and in the back of her mind she harbored some denial over the whole situation. If only the team could win enough games, surely Dr. Prins would have a change of heart and welcome her husband back as head coach the following season. Eventually, the Mummes went to bed feeling great disappointment and mild denial.

The next morning Mumme called a meeting with the most trusted members of his coaching staff. Mike Fanoga, Mike Leach, Charlie Moot, John Wiley, and Marshall Cotton filed into the football office's meeting room and sat down at the conference table in the center of the room. Mumme began by explaining that he had a meeting with Dr. Prins after practice the previous afternoon and that the president had told him to go away when the season was over in November. The room absorbed the news in a protracted moment of stunned silence as each member of the staff waited for their head coach to offer some kind of plausible rationale for their dismissal. Mumme briefed them on the administration's flimsy justification that the football team was over budget and quickly moved forward, not wanting his coaches to dwell on the implications of the news he had just shared with them.

"Look," Mumme continued, "it would be better if no one knows about this." He pointed out that the team had already won three of the four most difficult games on the schedule. Winning out in the season's remaining games would likely put the Tigers in contention for a spot in the national playoffs, something that a football team at Iowa Wesleyan had never accomplished. If the coaching staff wanted to keep the team focused on their goals, the last thing the players needed to be thinking about was Mumme's firing. After all of the coaches agreed on this, they made a pact that word of Mumme's dismissal would not go beyond the room.

Before ending the meeting, Mumme relayed a final nugget of information from the previous day's meeting. "One more thing," he said, "Dr. Prins told me to tell you that all of you are welcome to apply for the football head coaching vacancy. Are any of you interested in the job?" Mumme's gaze went to his left, finding Mike Fanoga while the rest of the eyes in the room followed.

"No," said Fanoga with a simple shake of his head.

The room's attention moved to Leach, who proceeded to deliver an expletive-laced monologue that called out the administration for what he believed to be a "total sham power play." The soliloquy unequivocally settled the matter of his interest in the position of head football coach at Iowa Wesleyan: he wasn't. Leach finished by saying, "I wouldn't work for that son of a bitch if he was the last person on the face of the earth."

Wiley went next. He reiterated Leach's key points and let it be known that he had no desire to apply for the job. Cotton simply shook his head and laughed at the intrinsic absurdity of applying for a job with an institution that didn't find his boss's track record to be grounds for keeping his job.

This brought the floor to Moot. He proceeded to launch his own tirade against the injustice of Mumme's firing and may even have outdone Leach in sheer quantity of obscenities. However, he never said that he wasn't interested in the job. For someone with such a knack for survival, applying for the vacancy created by Mumme's dismissal certainly seemed to be a move that would be in character. It also didn't hurt that Moot genuinely enjoyed living in Mount Pleasant. He appreciated the close-knit community that he'd integrated himself into over the past year and a half, not to mention the old-school American values that the residents exhibited as they went about their everyday lives. Moot may have even gone so far as to consider them "tough." He didn't mind the slow pace of life and he enjoyed the familiarity that each day brought.

As the group got up from their seats and headed back to their desks, most figured that Moot would be submitting an application to Dr. Prins at some point. Any lingering doubts about Moot's vocational aspirations were obliterated when he showed up to the office in a coat and tie the next day, which turned out to be a fashion trend that continued for the rest of the season. The whole routine might have been infuriating if it wasn't so transparent.

After the meeting, things went smoother than one might expect from a team led by a lame duck coaching staff committed to throwing the football and whose starting quarterback was recovering from a torn rotator cuff. Thursday afternoon's practice session went off without a hitch as Dewald continued to run the offense by proxy through backup quarterback John Robinson. Meanwhile, the rest of the team was exceptionally focused on their jobs thanks to the unconventional quarterback situation. With Dewald's ability to perform in jeopardy, the veteran group recognized that it was each member of the team's responsibility to pick up the slack. When Iowa Wesleyan's homecoming game against Baker University rolled around on Saturday afternoon, the Tigers did not disappoint.

Defensively the Tigers were a force. The hard hitting-unit forced six Baker fumbles, recovered three of them, and snagged two interceptions on the day. Special teams also made a contribution, blocking a punt in the third quarter.

Offensively, Dewald spent the better part of the afternoon underthrowing his receivers thanks to the limitations presented by his torn rotator cuff. His arm was weak to begin with, but a couple hours before game time the pain in his shoulder was so bad that he couldn't bear to throw during warm-ups. To ease the pain, Dewald took a cortisone shot that combined with the adrenaline of kickoff to make throwing bearable when it was time for him to run Iowa Wesleyan's offense.

Although the shot masked the pain, it couldn't do anything to restore the strength to Dewald's shoulder. Any ball he threw that traveled more than 30 yards looked like a crappy punt as it hung in the air for what seemed like an eternity. Fortunately, that gave his receivers plenty of time to camp out underneath the ball and outwork Baker's defensive backs for position. The inspired play of the receiving corps was led by Bruce Carter, himself returning from a sprained ankle, who managed to catch 10 passes for 74 yards in the first action he'd seen in two weeks. Thanks to the receivers' aggressive play in the passing game, Dewald's stat line at the end of the game suggested that he was in top form: 39 completions on 52 attempts for 321 yards and five touchdowns. The end result was a 42–14 win for the Tigers, and the lopsided score allowed for Dewald and Carter to get a much-needed rest during the fourth quarter. The collaborative nature of the victory was complemented by the fact that eleven different Iowa Wesleyan receivers caught passes on the day. It was a true team win.

The following week, the Tigers put forth another solid team effort to win a tough match up against perpetual rival, Greenville College, 30–14. The Illinois school had played a part in preventing the Tigers from winning conference championships in each of the previous two seasons, and for the graduating members of the team, it was their final opportunity to get a win against the Panthers. Making the outcome even sweeter for Mumme was the knowledge that he finally had gotten the best of his former colleague from the University of Texas at El Paso, Greenville head coach Max Bowman. The fact that Bowman had kept Iowa Wesleyan on the schedule when the majority of the Illini-Badger-Hawkeye Conference had dropped them spoke volumes about the mutual respect the coaches shared for one another. Even so, that respect didn't make the 16-point road victory any less sweet for Mumme or his players.

Iowa Wesleyan continued its winning ways a week later when it bestowed a 55–3 thrashing on former conference opponent, Lakeland College in Sheboygan, Wisconsin. Dewald's arm was starting to feel better on game days, and his mental reps at the helm of the Tigers' offense on practice days were beginning to feel routine. Meanwhile, the rest of the team was rising to the challenge of heightened expectations, exemplified best by the continued emergence of Iowa Wesleyan's smothering defense. While Mumme's offense continued to garner headlines and the undivided attention of the crowds wherever it played, Moot's defense was consistently, if not discreetly, delivering stellar performances week after week. The higher level of intensity on both sides of the ball began to make the team believe that they could very well be in the middle of the march to a national championship.

12

TRAGEDY

Wednesday, October 16, 1991, started off typically enough. Roommates Dustin Dewald and Robert Draper left home in the morning and headed off to their respective academic obligations. Draper went to Iowa Wesleyan's campus for class, and Dewald made his way to Mount Pleasant High School for another day of student teaching. Early in the afternoon, the pair came home to grab a bite to eat and a couple hours of rest before going back to campus for football practice. On walking through the door, the two of them flopped onto the couch and turned on the TV to see a "Breaking News" Bulletin. A somber broadcaster delivered the news that a gunman had opened fire at the Luby's Cafeteria in Killeen, Texas, a town of 100,000 just ten miles east of Copperas Cove where Dewald, Draper, and a number of their teammates had grown up and played high school football for Mumme. Details trickled out slowly as the body count began to rise with each update the television delivered. Panic officially began to set in when they learned that it was Bosses Day, and Draper recalled that his mother frequently went to Luby's for lunch with coworkers.

Draper and Dewald quickly began dialing every meaningful phone number that they could think of in a frantic effort to make sure that their loved ones were safe. In doing so, they joined a mass of people around the country who were trying to get information out of Killeen that the television news couldn't provide on a developing tragedy. All the phone lines were jammed. Nonetheless, Dewald and Draper spent two hours pounding numbers on the phone and listening to the

121

exasperatingly obtuse recording on the other end of the line instructing them to hang up the phone and please try again. Without cell phones or the Internet at their disposal, they were forced to continue the maddeningly unproductive ritual and wait for updates from the television news until it was time to leave for practice.

Dewald, Draper, and other members of the team with roots in central Texas shared their concern and what little information they had with one another in the locker room and then on the practice field while they made a dubious effort to stay focused on football. Luby's was a popular dining spot, and it seemed that just about everyone had family and friends that ate there regularly. Everyone was starved for information about the developing story, and any details that someone provided quickly made the rounds throughout the team over the course of practice. As with any game of telephone, by the time those details got back around to the originator it was an entirely different story and it was subsequently passed on as such. For anyone with loved ones near Killeen, Wednesday's practice turned out to be two of the most frustrating hours of their young lives.

Word eventually got to Mumme and the rest of the coaching staff what was going on back at home for a good portion of the roster. When Mumme addressed the team to end practice, he acknowledged the situation in Killeen and informed his players that anyone who had been affected by the days' events was free to go home and tend to any matters that required their attention. At that point, nobody knew much of anything, so when practice broke most of the team raced back to their dorm rooms, apartments, and houses to learn whatever they could about what exactly had happened in Killeen. When they got home, a clearer picture of the tragedy began to emerge.

At 12:45 P.M. that afternoon, deranged loner George Hennard, Jr., drove his Ford Ranger through a plate glass window at the front of the restaurant. Before even getting out of his truck, Hennard began opening fire on patrons. For the next ten minutes, armed with two 9-mm semiautomatic pistols, Hennard calmly strode about the restaurant and carried out cold-blooded executions while patrons hid underneath tables or whatever cover they could find. One man even threw his body through a plate glass window that allowed dozens of other people to escape. When law enforcement finally arrived on the scene and drove the gunman to turn his weapon on himself, he had killed twenty-three people and wounded twenty-seven more. At the time, it was the deadliest massacre in US history.

Somewhere amid the horrific details that came out that evening, Dewald and Draper were finally able to reach their families and learn that they were safe.

However, as news stations began to report the names of the victims a number of them hit home.

Dr. Michael Griffith, forty-eight years old, was a neighbor, friend, and veterinarian to the Dewald family. Griffith had tried to come to the gunman's aid when he first crashed through the front of the restaurant. He was the day's first victim.

Al Gratia was the second name that Dewald recognized. Dewald had played golf with him a number of times at the Hills of Cove Golf Course in scrambles and community fundraisers. Despite being seventy years old, Gratia heroically charged the shooter in an effort to disarm him after a man threw himself through the plate glass window. His actions provided the diversion that dozens of people needed to escape, including his daughter, Suzanna Gratia Hupp. Gratia's wife Ursula was killed when she rushed to her husband's side rather than escaping.

Dewald was hardly the only member of the team who was touched by the tragedy. Wide receiver Chann Chavis lost one of his high school teachers in the shooting. One of the school board members that Mumme had worked with in his time at Copperas Cove was also killed.

The collective heartbreak of the team was palpable the next day at practice. Mumme reiterated to his players that they were free to go home and grieve with their loved ones if they had been affected by the previous days' events. Nearly a dozen players took him up on the offer and headed home to be with their families if they hadn't already done so. Dewald, Draper, and Chavis were among those who stayed on campus and did their best to care about football. Dewald found strength by spending what time he could on the phone with Tiffany, who was back in Copperas Cove living with her family and teaching, talking about their shared anguish and their heartbroken hometown. By the time he got into bed on Friday night, he was feeling prepared to travel to Jacksonville, Illinois, the following morning to lead his team against MacMurray College.

That feeling was shattered when the phone rang well after midnight. It was Tiffany. Local police had just come to her door to inform the family that her brother Mark, who lived in Austin, had been shot. That was all that she knew. Tiffany and her family were getting ready to pile into the car and begin driving south to be with Mark at the hospital. Dewald spent the next couple of hours pacing by the phone waiting for another update from his wife.

The phone rang again around 4 A.M. with awful news. Earlier that day, Mark had been packing for a road trip from Austin to Little Rock, to watch the

University of Texas play the University of Arkansas along with his roommate. He insisted on packing his 9 mm in light of the events that had taken place in Killeen. At some point while he and his roommate were packing for the trip a bullet accidentally discharged from the gun and struck Mark in the head. Dewald was stunned. He spent the rest of the conversation doing what he could to comfort his wife as he struggled to manage his own shock over the news.

When Dewald hung up the phone he immediately picked it up again to dial his parents. He needed to get to Austin to be with his wife and her family. His parents were planning to fly from Austin to St. Louis that morning so that they could make the drive to Jacksonville, Illinois, for the MacMurray game that afternoon. He wanted to be with his wife more than anything, but skipping the game was not a viable option logistically and he didn't want to abandon his teammates. Dewald would have to wait until after the game to return to Texas with his family and be with his wife.

Dewald arrived on campus Saturday morning to board the bus to Illinois a few minutes late. He immediately sought out Mumme to explain the situation and to inform him that he wouldn't be joining the team for the bus ride back to Mount Pleasant following the game. He wasn't sure when he would return to the team, and between his sleep deprivation and grief, he was in no state to sort through those kinds of details.

The three-hour bus ride to Jacksonville was a haze. His last conversation with his wife had been hours ago, and in the few brief moments of clarity that Dewald had on the bus and during his pregame routine he wondered what he was doing playing football at a time like this. His hometown was in disarray over the senseless massacre in neighboring Killeen only three days ago and his adopted family's collective heart had been shattered as his brother-in-law was on life support. For the first time in his life, a football game felt utterly meaningless. When the national anthem began to play before kickoff and Dewald finally had two still minutes to himself, he finally broke down.

He wasn't alone. Iowa Wesleyan's roster was filled with guys who called the area around Killeen home. They were all nursing fresh wounds from a week of tragedy and they were all searching for some kind of motivation to play a football game in Illinois while their hearts were with their community in Texas. Somehow they found it, and the defense overwhelmed MacMurray's offense as the team coasted to an easy 31–0 win despite an uncharacteristically shaky performance from Dewald.

After showering in the locker room, Dewald gathered some things and joined his family as they raced to the St. Louis Airport to board a flight for Austin. He got to the hospital in time to find his anguished wife Tiffany approaching the doors. The tears streaming down her face said everything. Mark had just passed. After a long embrace, she told her husband that there wasn't any hope for Mark from the start, but her family chose to wait to take her brother off life support so that they could donate his organs to save somebody else's life. Dewald spent the next few hours in a catatonic state, overcome by exhaustion and grief as he did all that he could to support his wife and her family in a time of unspeakable angst.

Back in Mount Pleasant, there was little question in Mumme's mind as to how he should handle his quarterback's absence. Dewald hadn't taken a practice snap since he tore his rotator cuff during the Harding game. In the games that followed the injury, Iowa Wesleyan had gone 4–0 and scored 158 points: if Dewald was in uniform the following Saturday, he would start at quarterback against Wayne State. Despite Charlie Moot's usual objections to starting a player who hadn't practiced, Mumme informed the rest of the coaching staff and the team that Dewald would be the starter that week if he could make it back to Mount Pleasant for game time.

When his focus wasn't on the players who were actually on the practice field, Mumme spent the week doing all that he could to prepare Dewald for Saturday's game despite the thousand miles between them. He sent VHS tapes of Wayne State's game film overnight to Copperas Cove so that Dewald could get a feel for their defense when he wasn't tending to family matters. The combination of grainy secondhand tapes and the VCR didn't provide Dewald with a particularly clear viewing experience. Mumme told his quarterback to be mindful of Wayne State's inside linebacker who was an imposing physical presence and a speedy defensive back. The scouting report wasn't helpful because Dewald couldn't even tell who was who thanks to the poor quality of the film. Nonetheless, the tapes offered a welcome diversion in the midst of a week filled with sadness.

Mumme and Dewald also logged plenty of time on the phone together over the course of the week. Neither had much to say about football during these conversations, so they talked about life and Mumme did his best to offer some comfort during what he could only imagine was the most trying time in Dewald's life. It was difficult for Mumme to find the words to console Dewald because they felt so puny in comparison to the magnitude of his struggle. The two of them shared about as close a personal relationship as a coach and a player could.

Mumme had known Dustin and Tiffany since they were in high school, and Tiffany had spent her two years at Iowa Wesleyan working as Mumme's secretary. His heart ached for both of them.

On Friday afternoon, Dewald was a pallbearer at Mark's funeral. After the service, Dewald, his parents, and his brother headed to the airport to board a red-eye flight to St. Louis. In need of a change in scenery after an agonizing ten days in Texas, Tiffany and her brother Jeff joined the Dewalds for the trip. On arriving in St. Louis, the six of them made the three-and-a-half-hour drive to Mount Pleasant, arriving early Saturday morning. Dewald got a couple hours of sleep before heading to Mapleleaf Field at 10 A.M., just four hours before the afternoon's scheduled kickoff.

He headed straight to the field for the team's walkthrough and also to let Mumme know that he was available to play if he was needed. Mumme was relieved to see him because he hadn't been sure that Dewald would make it back to Mount Pleasant in time for kickoff. After the walkthrough, Mumme took a moment to express his condolences for Dewald's loss. Then Mumme told Dewald that he would be starting and offered a few words of encouragement that may have been a touch indelicate. "I don't want to put any more pressure on you," he began, "but if we don't win this game we're not going to make the playoffs." In the big picture, Iowa Wesleyan's march to the playoffs probably didn't mean a whole lot in that moment, but Mumme's comment served as a reminder that Dewald had just returned to place where that goal was paramount. Dewald responded in typical fashion, shrugging his shoulders and telling his coach not to worry about it and that he had the situation under control.

Despite the painful week he'd spent at home in Texas, Dewald found himself feeling much more confident and comfortable than he had the week before as he suited up in the locker room. That may have had something to do with the fact that this game didn't have the same air of uncertainty as the previous week's game at MacMurray. Although there had been a painful resolution to the situation in Mark's passing, it did provide Dewald with a sense of closure. There was nothing left to do but begin the healing process, and for Dewald that meant picking apart a defense with the help of his friends on Iowa Wesleyan's sideline. Dewald also found strength in the kind words of condolence and support that trickled in from his teammates in the locker room and throughout pregame warm-ups.

The skies were grey at kickoff and a perpetual drizzle fell throughout the game. The slippery conditions proved to be costly on Iowa Wesleyan's first possession when a receiver slipped, allowing Dewald's pass to fall into the hands of the cornerback Mumme had spent the week warning him about. Moot took the opportunity to pounce on Mumme, chasing him down the sideline to say "I told you so" to which Mumme responded, "Shut up, just stop 'em." After a long interception return, Wayne State's offense took over and ran the ball into the end zone a few plays later for a 7–0 lead. It would be their final lead of the afternoon.

Once the miscue on the game's first series was behind them, Dewald and Iowa Wesleyan's offense dominated. Dewald capped the ensuing possession with a 3-yard touchdown pass to Bruce Carter and never looked back. The Tigers scored another touchdown on a one yard run for a 14–7 lead at the end of the first quarter. The domination continued as Dewald delivered a 5-yard touchdown pass to Rich Morrow to start the second quarter before throwing another to Marcus Washington before the first half came to a close with Iowa Wesleyan holding a 28–10 lead.

The offense picked up where it left off when it returned to the field for the third quarter. The Tigers spent the third quarter moving the chains and scoring points as Sean Morris, Dana Holgorsen, and Chris Oepping hauled in touchdowns from Dewald. Meanwhile, the defense continued to play its suffocating brand of football on the strength of a dominating performance by the defensive line. When Dewald threw a 66-yard touchdown pass to Carter early in the fourth quarter to give the Tigers a 55–17 advantage, Mumme figured he'd seen all he needed to see from his embattled quarterback and pulled him from the game.

When Dewald got to the bench, he'd thrown for 507 yards and seven touchdowns, both school records. Teammates and coaches came by to offer words of congratulations and condolence as the game clock dwindled. Later, Dewald's father made it down to the field to grab his son by the shoulder and let him know how proud he was of the performance he'd just delivered in the face of overwhelming adversity and the man that he was revealing himself to be. After a moment, the elder Dewald headed back to the stands to rejoin his family and leave his son be.

As he sat on the bench, a flood of emotion washed over Dewald. It was the first moment he had to himself to be alone where he wasn't required to carry some kind of weight. From trying to be strong in the aftermath of the Luby's shooting or carrying his brother-in-law's casket only the day before, he'd spent ten days as a veritable emotional forklift. After all of that, he had to get motivated for a football game to keep his team in the playoff hunt. As he sat there, Dewald couldn't ignore all the ways that his world had irrevocably changed in the past week and a half

127

any longer. It didn't matter that he was only twenty-three, his experiences were a load that would have been difficult for anyone to handle.

That's why Dewald, after delivering the finest performance of his college career in a game that kept Iowa Wesleyan's football team firmly in the national playoff picture, spent the final seconds of a 55–32 victory sitting alone on the bench, weeping.

13

A PLAYOFF RUN FROZEN

The emotionally battered Tigers' dismantling of Wayne State brought their record on the season to 8–1 and propelled them to sixth place nationally in the NAIA Division I rankings. The résumé the team had accumulated over the course of the season was impressive, but with two games remaining on their schedule there was plenty of work to be done. Because Iowa Wesleyan competed as an independent, they wouldn't have an automatic bid or the support of a conference when the selection committee decided which eight teams would advance to the national playoffs. Consequently, the Tigers didn't just need to win their last two games to ensure themselves a chance to win a national championship, they needed to dominate.

Iowa Wesleyan's next scheduled contest with Blackburn College didn't constitute much of a roadblock. The Beavers were 0–7 coming into the game and the Tigers had outscored them by a combined margin of 96–32 the previous two seasons. After a shaky first quarter at Mapleleaf Field, the 1991 iteration of the lopsided match up proved to be more of the same. The Tigers took a 32–0 lead into the locker room at halftime and cruised the rest of the way for a 59–7 victory. Dewald threw for 387 yards and seven touchdowns on the afternoon, three to Bruce Carter, two to Marcus Washington, as well one apiece to Dana Holgorsen and Chann Chavis. The defense delivered another stellar performance, holding Blackburn to 138 yards of total offense.

Seemingly, the win brought Iowa Wesleyan a step closer to the playoffs, however, that wasn't exactly the case. Somehow, the national poll released a day after the game dropped the Tigers two positions to eight, which left their spot in the playoff picture unclear. Iowa Wesleyan would need another convincing victory to make a compelling argument for their inclusion in the national playoffs. Their final opportunity to do so was a showdown with the same Concordia team that had dashed the Tigers' dreams of a conference championship a year before. Concordia came to Mapleleaf Field with virtually the same team that had beaten Iowa Wesleyan 31–28 in the 1990 season finale, which was just fine by Mumme. The opportunity for revenge made the season's final game a personal grudge match for the majority of the roster.

Dewald and the Tigers' offense got the scoring started with a 22-yard touchdown pass to Carter on their first play from scrimmage. It was a good indication of the slugfest that was to come that afternoon at Mapleleaf Field. The two teams took turns lighting up the scoreboard on their next four possessions, and when the first quarter came to a close, Iowa Wesleyan held a 19–13 lead thanks to three touchdown passes from Dewald to Carter.

The scoring slowed some in the second quarter, but not much. With Iowa Wesleyan holding a 25–20 lead and the ball on the Falcons' 22-yard line with one second remaining in the half, Mumme chose to let Dewald air it out one more time instead of kicking a field goal into the wind. It was a wise decision. Dewald threw his fourth touchdown pass to Carter, his fifth of the afternoon, on the ensuing play for a 33–20 advantage going into the half.

When play resumed after the intermission, Concordia took control of the game. Their defense managed to stifle Dewald and the rest of the offense for the next fifteen minutes while the Falcons' offense chipped away at the Tigers' lead by putting up nine points in the quarter. At the end of three quarters, Concordia was within striking distance. In his final quarter of play at Mapleleaf Field, Dewald and the rest of the Tigers put that notion to bed.

In the ensuing fifteen minutes, Dewald threw two touchdowns and ran for another as Iowa Wesleyan scored 26 points. Meanwhile, the defense found its rhythm and held Concordia scoreless, giving the Tigers a 59–29 victory and a 10–1 regular season record. The team had made its case on the field for a bid to the national playoffs by hanging 50 points on each of their final three opponents. In doing so, Dewald threw for 22 touchdowns and more than 1,300 yards while the Tigers outscored the opposition 174–68. With a week to go before the selection committee chose which teams would advance to the playoffs, it was time for Mumme to get to work making sure that his team's case was well known.

For Mumme, that meant spending the week working the phones virtually every minute that he wasn't on the practice field. For the next six days, Mumme talked to every NAIA Division I head coach with a vote that would take his call and presented Iowa Wesleyan's case for a higher ranking. One coach who was sympathetic to his plight was William "Billy" Joe who had a built a powerhouse of his own at Central State University in Ohio. Joe had led the Marauders to a national championship in 1990 and would do so again in the 1992 season. Impressed with their résumé, he championed Iowa Wesleyan's cause to fellow voters and even voted the Tigers first in the nation on his final ballot.

In the midst of getting out the word of his team's impressive season, there was another piece of emerging news that Mumme had spent most of the season trying to keep under wraps. Rumors had begun circulating around Mount Pleasant that he wouldn't be returning to Iowa Wesleyan's sidelines for the 1992 season. The previous week a number of booster club members caught wind of those rumors and began handing out petitions to local businesses for members of the community to sign in support of Mumme and the coaching staff. Although no one was willing to give any public credibility to those rumors, they still made for stories that landed on the front page of the sports section in local newspapers. Headlines like "Petitions circulated to support Mumme" and "Statement leaves Mumme's status unclear" led to rampant speculation that Mumme would be on his way out of town at season's end. It was the last thing he wanted to deal with as he tried to keep the team focused while they waited to learn the fate of their season.

Fortunately, over the course of the season the team had proven itself to be skillful in tuning out distractions when it came time to hit the field. The vast majority of the players found no trouble ignoring the rumors that Mumme's tenure as head coach at Iowa Wesleyan was coming to an end. Plus, it didn't make a whole lot of sense to fire a coach who had just led the football program to its first ten-win season in school history. What were the odds?

By the time the following Sunday rolled around, there wasn't anything left to do but wait. Mumme had spent the week pleading his case to anyone who was willing to listen and he kept his players limber by having them hit the practice field three times over the course of the week. The votes were in, and much of the team gathered in the football offices to find out whether or not they would make the playoffs. Optimism spread when the rankings came out and the Tigers leaped to seventh in the nation on the strength of Joe's placing Iowa Wesleyan first on his ballot. Nonetheless, they still had to wait for a phone call that would deliver the official word that they had made the playoffs. If the Tigers hadn't made the playoffs they would just wait around the office for a call that would never come.

Players and coaches had been hanging around Mumme's office waiting for what felt like an eternity when Mumme's phone finally rang. He picked up the phone to hear a member of the NAIA Playoff's selection committee on the other end of the line extending an invitation to the national playoffs. The grin that spread across Mumme's face instigated off a muffled celebration that escalated to full-fledged pandemonium when he hung up the phone. Players and coaches alike jumped up and down, yelled at the top of their lungs and smacked one another on the back as they all reveled in the moment created by reaching a goal that they had worked toward all season.

The Tigers would be traveling to Moorhead, Minnesota, a small town nearly six hundred miles north of Mount Pleasant, just across the North Dakota border from Fargo. Waiting for Iowa Wesleyan in Minnesota in the national quarterfinals was fourth-ranked Moorhead State. Although the Tigers were hoping to host their first playoff game or travel south to conditions more favorable to their passing attack, the team was optimistic. The conditions weren't going to be optimal, but they figured Moorhead State would be little more than an icy step in their journey to a national championship.

Mumme knew better. Moorhead State had been a force all season, with their only loss coming against NCAA Division II opponent University of North Dakota. Offensively, the Dragons ran a potent triple-option attack that averaged nearly 280 yards rushing per contest, which was complimented by a capable passing game. On the other side of the ball, Moorhead State was equally proficient. The stingy defensive unit allowed 17 points per game and surrendered an average of 134 yards through the air. In a 30–26 victory over Southwest State of Minnesota toward the end of the season, the Dragons stymied NAIA Division I's leading passer Jeff Loots. Loots mustered only 203 yards through the air on 12 of 41 passing in the loss. Given the Dragons' recent performance, Mumme knew that Iowa Wesleyan could expect to take the field against a team that was just as confident as they were.

Thanks to an aggressive fundraising campaign that Mumme launched a week previously, the Tigers were able to fly to Minnesota for the Moorhead State game. At the conclusion of the regular season Mike Leach put together a highlight video featuring all forty-eight of Iowa Wesleyan's touchdown passes from the 1991 season set to John Cougar Mellencamp's "Small Town." Athletic director and assistant coach David Johnsen sent the highlight video along with a heartfelt letter asking for alumni support to send their alma mater's football team to the national playoffs. The response provided the funding necessary to fly the team along with some of the largest donors to Moorhead the following Friday.

When the plane touched down in Minnesota, the Tigers were taken directly to Alex Nemzek Stadium on Moorhead State's campus. When they arrived at the stadium, the team headed to the locker room to suit up for a walkthrough while Mumme went to make a brief appearance at a press conference. Once the press conference was over Mumme rejoined his team in the locker room to lead them onto the field to begin their walkthrough. As the coaches and players walked through the tunnel and began to approach the field they were hit with a gust of arctic air that made Mumme reconsider the afternoon agenda. He proceeded to weigh the value of a walkthrough in subzero temperatures against the idea of heading back into the locker room to get changed and check into a hotel that didn't feel like a breezy meat locker. Creature comforts won easily in a split-second decision. Mumme did an about face and told his team, "Alright guys, that's enough of that. Let's head back to the hotel."

After coaches and players had an opportunity to settle into their rooms, players, coaches, and support staff convened in one of the hotel banquet rooms for a team dinner. The Tigers were accompanied by a few generous donors who had contributed the funding to make flying to Minnesota possible as well as family members of different members of the coaching staff. As the meal went on, a number of players and coaches took the opportunity to stand up and thank the donors who had made the trip possible. Eventually those words of thanks led to words recognizing what the Tigers had accomplished that season in the face of some strong adversity. With rumors of Mumme's departure floating around town, a few players who had been paying attention to the news took the opportunity to say thank you for all the coaching staff had done over the past three years. It was a memorable evening, and although it was unintended, it ended up being goodbye.

The following morning the Tigers returned to the same banquet room for their pregame meal before heading to the stadium for their walkthrough. As much as they may have tried during warm-ups, once the team left the locker room there was no acclimating their bodies to the frigid temperatures that surrounded them. It wasn't as if Iowa Wesleyan didn't have experience playing in the elements. Their final two games of the season versus Blackburn and Concordia were played in steady winds and temperatures that were below 20 degrees, but this was different.

133

The temperature hovered around 0 degrees as a steady 20-mile-per-hour wind pounded away at their icy bodies.

The Tigers returned to the locker room of Alex Nemzek Stadium following a pregame routine that could hardly be considered a warm-up and made their final preparations for Moorhead State. Those preparations included the team gathering to recite a prayer that Marcus Washington brought to Iowa Wesleyan when he arrived on campus in August 1989. For the past three seasons Washington's prayer was a pregame ritual that the team carried on without fail before taking the field.

As the team gathered around one another for the prayer, every one of them reached out for a teammate. Some grabbed onto the shoulder pad in front of them, others held the hand next to them or locked arms or bowed their heads into one another as they took a knee to follow Washington's lead. Sixty-five players settled in to create the veritable calm before the storm when Washington's voice cut through the silence, "Lord, we thank you for this day."

Sixty-four young men collectively responded, "Lord, we thank you for this day."

"Grant us guidance in our play."
"Grant us guidance in our play."
"Give us strength in hands and heart."
"Give us strength in hands and heart."
"To the Fair in Sportsman Park."
"To the Fair in Sportsman Park."
"Courage, pride, and self-esteem."
"Courage, pride, and self-esteem."
"For our Tiger football team."
"For our Tiger football team."

"Amen," sixty-five voices said together, before rising to head out the locker room door and take the field against an imposing opponent with a trip to the national semifinals resting in the balance.

During the first quarter, Dewald and the offense struggled to get going as they fought against 30-mile-per-hour gusts of wind, frigid temperatures, and a tenacious Dragon defense. Meanwhile, outside of surrendering a 42-yard touchdown pass, the Tiger defense hung tough against Moorhead State's versatile offense. When the first quarter came to close with the Tigers down only six points and about to play the second quarter with the wind at their back, Iowa Wesleyan's sideline was confident they'd be able to turn the tide of the game in their favor. Even when

134

Moorhead State scored its second touchdown a minute into the second quarter, the Tigers were undeterred.

Down 12–0, the offense strode onto the field with the wind at their back and their sights set on the end zone. On the ensuing play, Dewald's pass over the middle was broken up by an official who couldn't get out of the way of the football. After two more incompletions, Iowa Wesleyan was forced to punt. The Dragons' offense responded by going 62 yards on 17 plays for a touchdown that brought the score to 18–0. Of equal consequence was the fact that the drive milked the clock of valuable time that the Tigers would be able to play with the wind at their back. Dewald would go on to comment after the game, "When we got the wind, I thought we'd be able to do whatever we wanted. Then all of a sudden there was four minutes left in the second quarter and we'd only take three snaps."

The ensuing kickoff return did little to help Iowa Wesleyan's cause. To counteract the high winds they were kicking into, Moorhead State's kicker booted a low line drive that came to a sudden stop on Iowa Wesleyan's 39-yard line. Unsure of what to do, some members of the Tigers' kickoff return team stared at the ball that lay just in front of them while others began to block members of Moorhead State's kickoff coverage unit as the ball lay just behind them. Whatever the reason, no Tiger player took assertive action to secure the football that lay on the ground nearby, and the Dragons recovered the kick. They scored six plays later and tacked on a two-point conversion for a 26–0 lead as only 2 minutes and 13 seconds remained in the half. For 10 and 1/2 minutes of play in the second quarter, Iowa Wesleyan's offense were little more than spectators, as the events on the field and a subzero wind chill pounded away at them.

Despite the rust, when the offense finally took the field, Dewald immediately got to work leading a drive that brought the Tigers to the Dragons' 30-yard line. Any renewed sense of optimism was immediately dashed when a Moorhead State linebacker intercepted a short pass from Dewald and ran it 72-yards into the end zone with little more than a minute to play in the half. Iowa Wesleyan headed to the locker room at the half in a 34–0 hole. With the weather conditions being what they were, the game may as well have been over. However, if the 1991 season revealed anything about the Tigers' it's that quitting wasn't in their DNA. The team returned to the field after the intermission and played a gritty second half amid freezing temperatures and bone-chilling wind gusts. Iowa Wesleyan managed to score touchdowns in the third and fourth quarters, but it wasn't enough to overcome the first-half deficit; the final score was 47–14. If the Tigers were the type of team to search for moral victories, the second-half score may have provided some solace, but players of that persuasion hit the bricks when Mumme arrived on campus three years before.

What the team had the hardest time getting past was the feeling that they had been cheated. Their season was supposed to end in two weeks as they hoisted a trophy over their heads. After all that they'd been through over the course of the season, a national championship seemed to be their destiny. The loss brought an end to the season for everyone associated with Iowa Wesleyan's football program. For many of the players who undressed in the visitors' locker room at Alex Nemzek Field that day, it would be the last time that they would ever wear a football uniform. It didn't seem right that their team full of Texans, Floridians, and Samoans had to travel 580 miles north to play in 0-degree weather with 30-mile-per-hour winds against a rush-oriented opponent with a roster full of players from Minnesota and North Dakota. It wasn't fair that their quarterback had to throw into strong winds in frigid temperatures all afternoon as he recovered from a torn rotator cuff. The entire afternoon was a wash, and there was little any of them could do about it. As the team had learned all too well in the wake of the Luby's massacre, sometimes life can be maliciously unfair. It was a painful lesson to have reinforced so suddenly.

Mumme tried to offer his players whatever solace he could as they prepared to head to the airport for the flight back to Mount Pleasant, but it was a difficult sell. He shared the team's hurt and there was nothing that he could do to alleviate the palpable sense of disappointment that hung in the locker room as the team took its pads off one last time. To make matters worse, Mumme knew that he would be returning to a town where he no longer had a job.

14

COMEDY IN HINDSIGHT

According to Carol Burnett, "Comedy is tragedy plus time." The days and weeks that followed Iowa Wesleyan's loss to Moorhead State seemed to have all the components of a tragedy. Disappointment of goals left unfulfilled wasn't alleviated by the optimism that usually arises after the season's final games begin to fade in the rearview mirror. There was not going to be a collective shift in focus among the coaching staff toward the possibilities of next autumn. No one was scouring film in search of talented athletes to bring to Mount Pleasant in the future, there weren't any looming recruiting visits, and nobody was planning offseason fundraising events. That's because Mumme and his coaching staff had known for two months that come January 1 they were out of a job. Any of Mumme's frustration associated with the season's premature conclusion quickly took backseat to the anxiety of not knowing how he was going to provide for his family come the new year. It was a sentiment shared by several members of Iowa Wesleyan's lame-duck coaching staff.

The five weeks of vocational purgatory that ensued after the Moorhead State loss and before the staff's unemployment probably would have been a lot more painful if they hadn't been so awkward. On the advice of counsel, Mumme and his coaching staff continued to show up at the office every day and pretended to work. "He didn't fire you, he just told you to go away," Mumme's lawyer explained. "And he did it in a pretty bad way." Despite college president Dr. Robert Prins' request that Mumme take his business elsewhere after the season and his threat to stop paying him at the end of the year, the fact remained that the coach and the school still had a contract. So long as he continued to show up for work every day, the college was legally obligated to pay him. Whether or not Iowa Wesleyan would actually continue to cut him a check was a different matter entirely, but Mumme's presence in the office each day made a compelling case in his favor if the matter were to ever end up in a courtroom. As the clock counting down to coaching staff's ouster at Iowa Wesleyan continued to tick, Mumme sat in his office, working the phones in a timed search for an opportunity that would provide him and his assistant coaches continued employment.

In addition to conducting a job search, Mumme spent his time in the office counseling his former players as to what their next move should be. Although the school had yet to make an official statement regarding Mumme's employment status for the following season, those in the know were well aware that he would not be returning for the 1992 season. While the eligibility clock had expired for players like Dustin Dewald, Marcus Washington, and several more, there were a number of others who had yet to finish their collegiate playing careers. Players like Dana Holgorsen, Bill Bedenbaugh, York Kurinsky, and many more had to decide whether or not they wanted to continue their playing careers at Iowa Wesleyan under a new head coach.

Mumme did his best to put his feelings about the college aside and consider each player's unique situation to point them in a direction that would be most beneficial for their playing career and future aspirations. As painful as it was, this was the part of Mumme's role during this peculiar time period that was most rewarding. Even though Iowa Wesleyan's administration was in the process of stripping Mumme of his official coaching duties, his former players still sought his advice on what to do in a difficult situation. It was an acknowledgement that he would always be their coach in some way, even if his job title didn't explicitly say so.

Then there was the mole. Everyone involved in the meeting two months prior in which Mumme revealed his impending dismissal to his coaching staff assumed that Charlie Moot would go after the job. No one suspected how strangely that pursuit would play out during their final days at Iowa Wesleyan. As Moot continued his routine of arriving to work each morning in a coat and tie, he gradually began to take on a more and more authoritative demeanor among the other members of the coaching staff. During the season Moot had treated each day as if it were another interview for the head coaching job. He dressed for the part and minded his manners in the presence of administrators while carrying out his duties as defensive coordinator. With the season over and players leaving campus for Christmas break, Mumme lost the power invested in him by the collective confidence and support of a loyal roster. Sensing the vacancy that was gradually being created at the top of the power structure of the football program, Moot decided that he was going to conduct himself as Iowa Wesleyan's head coach until a recognized authority figure informed him otherwise. As one might expect, the silent coup went over about as well as a root canal among the rest of Iowa Wesleyan's coaching staff, who Moot had begun treating as his subordinates.

The growing tide of resentment generated by Moot's commandeering a not-quite vacant head coaching position finally came to its breaking point on a trip the entire staff took to the American Football Coaches Association Convention in Dallas. Mumme flew to the convention while the rest of the coaching staff drove, creating a power vacuum, which afforded Moot the perfect opportunity to assert authoritarian measures. He made it clear to the entire coaching staff that while they were at the convention, each of them would be on a budget and all expenses over the course of the trip were to be approved by him. The new policies and the implicit suggestion that Moot was now somehow authorized to make these types of decisions drew plenty of eye rolls from the rest of the coaching staff. Mike Leach decided that he'd seen Moot buy beer with his Iowa Wesleyan issued gas card too many times to quietly accept the financial shackles being placed on him. "You're not the head coach," he finally fired back, "and I don't work for you." The act of defiance did little to curtail Moot's authoritarian approach to managing what he believed to be his coaching staff. It did, however, put Moot on notice that he ought to spend the weekend searching for an offensive coordinator if he planned on being Iowa Wesleyan's head coach because Leach surely would not be sticking around.

As Moot's actions as make-believe head coach grew bolder and the rest of the coaching staff grew more resentful, Dr. Prins spent his time leading a string of head coaching candidates through Iowa Wesleyan's football offices while he interviewed them for Mumme's job. It was a cold-blooded thing to do, but it was the type of passive aggressive move Mumme figured he could expect from an administration that still refused to admit that he had been fired. The administration's public comments in the two months since Mumme was told to move on were cryptic. As rumors regarding Mumme's employment swirled around town along with petitions in favor of it, Prins would only say, "The college realizes that due to the success of the program, other opportunities may become available to him."

When given the opportunity to discuss his situation with men who were interviewing for his job, Mumme was far less ambiguous about the reasons for his departure. He explained that his teams had gone 24–11 over the course of three seasons in Mount Pleasant with a roster that he'd built from scratch after the program spent four years embarrassing itself because it ran its last successful coach out of town too. If they were to take the job, Mumme explained, they would essentially be walking into a career black hole.

Mumme's words were honest, but they were also meant to serve another purpose, which was to scare off prospective applicants to ensure that Charlie Moot would succeed him as head coach. Despite the unbecoming manner in which Moot was pursuing Mumme's job, he still had the support of most of his fellow coaches, even if they weren't all that interested in working under him. Sure, Moot's pursuit of the job hadn't been the most diplomatic endeavor and, yes, it probably would have helped his popularity if he'd been more forthcoming with his intentions from the beginning. But after two years in close quarters with the man, the rest of the coaching staff recognized that it was unreasonable to expect Moot to navigate a delicate situation with anything resembling tact. The man was a social lummox, and that was one of his most endearing qualities. He may have brought Leach, Mike Fanoga, Mumme, and the rest of the staff to their wit's end during an incredibly frustrating time in their lives, but they still wanted the best for their colleague and friend.

Although Mumme spent the majority of his time in the office searching for a new job and discouraging outside hires from pursuing his current job, he also did a fair amount of campaigning on Moot's behalf. Those activities primarily consisted of Mumme rallying support for Moot within Iowa Wesleyan's booster club. John Wright, Bob Lamm, and the rest of the usual suspects let the college know that they wanted Moot to be named head coach. They figured it was Iowa Weselyan's best chance to maintain the unprecedented success of the past three years. On the strength of their endorsement, Moot was soon tabbed to be Iowa Wesleyan's next head football coach.

Although Mumme was successful in ensuring Moot's ascension to head coach, he found the matters pertaining to his own employment to be a more difficult nut to crack. He spent the month of December talking with athletic directors all over the country, and even found himself deep into a number of head coaching searches across the country. University of South Dakota and Missouri Western State University both expressed serious interest in bringing Mumme on as their next head football coach before ultimately deciding to go in a different direction. However, the most serious interest came from a high school south of Dallas in Bryan, Texas.

Travis Bryan III, flew Mumme and his wife June into town to take a tour of the local high school's campus and athletic facilities as well as get acquainted with the community. Bryan's father had selected the outgoing head football coach twenty years before, and two decades later the son was taking it on himself to find the next one. Bryan explained to Mumme that he was the leading candidate after a nationwide search that he had conducted to find the next football coach of Bryan High School. It seemed that the job would be his if he wanted it, and as the Mummes flew back to Mount Pleasant after the visit, they felt as if they were finally out of the woods.

It would never come to pass. While Mumme was being wooed by one booster, another member of the school board had been conducting their own search for a head coach. Mumme ultimately learned of the parallel coaching searches after he returned to Mount Pleasant and was informed that he would not be the next head coach at Bryan High School. It was back to the drawing board. With Christmas and unemployment only days away, it was difficult news to digest. His final day in the office would be no more merciful.

Being the tight-knit community that it was, Iowa Wesleyan gave turkeys to all of its full-time employees to help celebrate the holidays. It was a symbol of familiarity and warmth between its giver and recipient, an acknowledgement that the college and its employees were celebrating Christmas together in some small way. The sight of them made Mumme want to puke. He felt he was losing his job for spite and none of the perpetrators of the injustice were even willing to admit what was happening. He felt no sense of affection for Iowa Wesleyan's administration, and it was clear that the feeling was mutual on their end as well. Mumme would be willing to starve before he would take that godforsaken bird home with him to feed his family.

Early in the afternoon, an assistant from the president's office came into Mumme's office to deliver an envelope. "What's this?" he asked the messenger. The assistant shrugged, turned and raced out of Mumme's office like someone had just pulled the fire alarm. Mumme opened the envelope to find a paycheck and a handwritten note from Dr. Prins indicating that the paycheck would be his last from Iowa Wesleyan. This seemed like a good point for Mumme to call it a day. He gathered his personal effects and headed out of the office one last time. Behind him he heard someone call out, "Coach, don't forget your Christmas turkey." He responded with the least offensive action he could think of, which was to continue on a deliberate path out of the building and head straight home.

An hour later, Moot showed up on Mumme's doorstep with the unclaimed Christmas turkey under one arm. Underneath the other arm he carried a six-pack of beer. He was bringing a knife to a gun fight. Mumme had just gotten into his third glass of bourbon, and the sight of the naked bird's corpse left him incensed. Without uttering a syllable, Mumme snatched the turkey from Moot's grasp and began trudging down the street through a fresh blanket of snow with the turkey over his right shoulder like a serving tray. Moot watched Mumme stomp off and realized he was headed in the direction of Dr. Prins' house, which was only a couple doors down the street. "Hey!" Moot called out. "What are you doing?" He proceeded to follow Mumme down the street as fast as he could, shouting "Hal!" and "Hold on!" all along the way in a fruitless effort to thwart what seemed to be an inevitable act of vandalism.

However, Mumme had no intention of the sort. He planned on making a statement. When he reached the fence enclosing Prins' front yard, he leaned back and launched the flightless bird as far as it had ever traveled through the air in its entire miserable existence. The turkey landed a couple feet short of the front step and sat in the snow, waiting to be discovered by Dr. Prins whenever he came home. Mumme figured that Dr. Prins could figure out who had put it there and their motivation for doing so without much difficulty. Satisfied, he walked back to his house feeling cathartic about the whole experience as he stared down a shocked Charlie Moot.

The next morning Mumme walked into his front yard to retrieve the morning paper. Curious to see whether or not yesterday's "statement" had been discovered, he grabbed his paper and moseyed a little ways down the street to catch a glimpse of the Prins' front lawn. The turkey was gone. Leading up to and away from the spot where it had been lying were Moot's size-nine footprints, which had probably been on a mission to preserve any shred of civility that may have remained between his past and hopefully future bosses. Then again, perhaps Moot was planning to put on a pot of turkey chili.

Whatever the motivation, Mumme couldn't help but shake his head and chuckle. His career was crumbling, and true to form, Moot was frantically scampering around town gathering the pieces so that he could redeem them for whatever they were worth.

15

MOVING ON

T hings didn't get any easier for Mumme or his family in the immediate aftermath of the turkey shot put. After the job at Bryan High School fell through in December, head coaching opportunities seemed to be nonexistent. A glimmer of hope was provided by a realtor from Valdosta, Georgia, who called Mumme's home to offer their services in finding a house. Confused, Mumme asked why a realtor from a thousand miles away would call him. The realtor responded, "You know you're a candidate for the job at Valdosta State College, right?"

Mike Leach practically begged Mumme to send his résumé to Valdosta when he learned that the school was searching for a new head coach. As it turned out, Leach supplemented the résumé with a highlight tape of Iowa Wesleyan's high-flying offense. The video was the same one that had been sent to Iowa Weselyan's boosters to raise money for the flight to Moorhead, Minnesota, a month before. It was one of many that he shipped to college programs across the country, but thus far it was the only one that had generated any tangible interest. It was encouraging, but a real estate agent acting on a tip from someone within the athletic department was hardly a call from an athletic director, so Mumme continued his search for work.

An opportunity came shortly after Christmas from Guy Morriss, head coach of the Washington Marauders of the upstart Professional Spring Football League (PSFL). Morriss told Mumme that the offensive coordinator job was his if he wanted it. The opportunity was a flimsy one. The league was high on hope and short on funding, so Mumme would have to pay for his plane ticket to the Marauders spring training in Orlando out of his own pocket. Nonetheless, it was an opportunity, and it was the only real one that Mumme had at the moment, so he boarded a flight for Orlando and left his family behind in Iowa in hopes that they would join him in Washington, D.C. when the regular season began.

For the next three weeks, Mumme lived out of a hotel room in Orlando along with defensive coordinator Rob Ryan. Morriss's room was just next door. The coaches spent their days at practice preparing the Marauders for the start of the PSFL season and their evenings in Morriss's hotel room talking football into the wee hours of the morning. Over the course of his three weeks in Orlando, Mumme was so focused on football that he failed to realize that he had not been paid by the Marauders until Ryan pointed out that only Morriss and the players had received paychecks.

Meanwhile, back on the farm, things in Mount Pleasant were on the verge of becoming contentious. After the new year, Dr. Prins followed through on his threat to stop paying Mumme's salary, leaving the family unsure of where money for groceries, heat, and mortgage payments would come from. June did her best to keep their household afloat while her husband toiled for a professional football team a thousand miles away that was on the brink of bankruptcy and Iowa Wesleyan refused to honor the contract they had given him only a year before. It was precisely the type of scenario she envisioned when she went on a three-month boycott of cooking for and speaking with Mumme after he left the sales job at his father's company to pursue a career in coaching.

Against this backdrop of financial distress and broken promises, Charlie Moot exercised his impeccable discretion and began pestering June for Iowa Wesleyan's game film from the previous season. As the leading contender for the theoretically vacant head coaching position at Iowa Wesleyan he figured that some game tape would be helpful to have on hand during the interview process. Moot assured June that Mumme had agreed to let him have the tapes. Her standard response to Moot's pursuit of the film was, "Do you have Hal's paycheck?" to which he would stammer about not wanting to get involved in those ugly bits and that the situation was out of his hands.

That may have been so, but Moot's good standing with the college made him the Mumme's only bridge to the administration. The fact remained that Mumme did not officially resign from his post as Iowa Wesleyan's head coach, the school had yet to formally fire him, and the two parties still had a contract that required the college to pay him. June remained steadfast in her demands, recognizing that the game film tucked underneath her bed was presently the family's most valuable bargaining chip if they hoped to get compensated by either of Mumme's two employers. She closed the matter by telling Moot that he could have the film when he delivered Hal's paycheck.

A few days later, Moot came to the Mumme's front door with Hal's paycheck from Iowa Wesleyan and June held up her end of the bargain by giving him the film that he needed. The money was enough to make another trip to the grocery store to feed the children for another week or two, but questions remained about where the family's next paycheck would come from. As January prepared to roll into February, the Mumme family's immediate economic future was looking awfully bleak.

However, just as the Marauders were making final preparations to travel to Washington, D.C. for their first preseason game, Mumme received a call from a member of the selection committee at Valdosta State asking him if he'd be interested in interviewing for the head coaching vacancy. "I understand you like to throw the ball," said a voice on the other end of line.

"Yes," replied Mumme, "but not until we get off the bus."

The rest of the conversation went well, and Mumme agreed to an interview and proceeded to drive three hours north to Valdosta to meet with the selection committee a couple days later. Mumme was skeptical that Valdosta State would actually offer him the job, so it came as a shock when he received a call a few days later from the athletic director asking him if he would be the next head football coach of the Blazers. As Mumme discovered much later, Valdosta State's athletic director had been captivated by the highlight film that Leach sent along as a supplement to Mumme's résumé. At night he showed his wife the tape of Iowa Wesleyan's forty-eight touchdown passes from the 1991 season and he would tell her, "I can sell this."

Before he accepted the offer, Mumme went to Morriss to inquire about his chances of getting paid. Morriss's response was philosophical. "This is a spring football league," Morriss began, "they're notorious about folding up. I don't think the state of Georgia is going to fold up." On that bit of insight, Mumme accepted the job at Valdosta State, drove north again for a press conference, and began to assemble a coaching staff.

Leach joined the coaching staff as offensive coordinator, Mike Major was brought back into the mix to be defensive coordinator, and Mumme saved a spot for Dana Holgorsen when he graduated from Iowa Wesleyan in May 1993. When the PSFL went belly up before opening day, Morriss came on as offensive line coach. From there, Mumme's offense and his coaching career promptly began to soar.

In five years at Valdosta State, Mumme posted a 40–17–1 record, made the national playoffs twice, and had two quarterbacks named finalists for the Harlon Hill Trophy. Chris Hatcher won the award in 1994 and Lance Funderburk was runner-up two years later. Over the course of his tenure, student enrollment grew from 6,500 to 10,000 and Valdosta State College became Valdosta State University. Then the SEC came calling.

When Kentucky hired Mumme as their head coach before the 1997 season, ringing endorsements for Mumme's coaching style and his offense immediately came from former players. Blazers wide receiver Sean Pender told the *Nashville Banner*, "If I could say one thing to the players at Kentucky, it would be this: Listen to Coach. Believe in him. Believe in his system. You will win." Tim Couch and the rest of the Wildcats offense quickly proved Pender a prophet when they beat Alabama for the first time in seventy-five years in 1997 and led the nation in passing. It wasn't a bad result for a school that finished 109 out of 111 Division I-A schools in total offense only a year before. In the next two seasons Kentucky appeared in back-to-back New Year's Day bowl games for the first time since Bear Bryant's postwar tenure in Lexington.

Mumme's success at Kentucky gave his offense, by then dubbed the Air Raid, a national stage. However, it was the success of the rest of Mumme's coaching tree that turned the system that he developed at Iowa Wesleyan into a full-fledged gridiron revolution.

After two years directing Mumme's offense at Kentucky, Leach accepted the offensive coordinator position at Oklahoma in January 1999. Following an abysmal 1998 season in which the Sooners' feeble offense managed to put up only seventeen points per game, Bob Stoops decided that he needed to hire Mumme's offense. It proved to be a wise decision. The Sooners averaged thirty-six points, and quarterback Josh Heupel passed for 3,850 yards, which was 1,700 more than any other quarterback in Oklahoma's storied history. The following season Oklahoma won a national championship and Heupel finished second in the Heisman Trophy voting while running the Air Raid. However, Leach was already gone by then.

Leach was named head coach at Texas Tech after the 1999 season and went on to have an unprecedented run of success in Lubbock. During his ten seasons with the Red Raiders, Leach took Texas Tech to ten bowl games and his teams led the nation in passing six times. He got to play pirate the entire time and remained confounded by the militant approach his contemporaries insisted on bringing to the football field. When discussing the Texas A&M student section, he famously quipped in 2005, "How come they get to pretend they are soldiers? The thing is, *they aren't actually in the military*. I ought to have Mike's Pirate School. The freshmen, all they get is the bandana. When you're a senior, you get the sword and skull and crossbones. For homework, we'll work on pirate maneuvers and stuff like that."

Most recently, Leach's metaphorical pirate ship has been flying the crimson and grey of Washington State University. True to form, the Cougars led the Pac-12 in passing during his first season in Pullman.

Dana Holgorsen was slow to come around on Mumme's gridiron vision, evidenced by his preference for English class over meeting with Iowa Wesleyan's new football coach in February 1989. However, when Holgorsen finally embraced Mumme's offensive philosophy, he found his calling. Holgorsen joined his former coaches in Georgia after he graduated from Iowa Wesleyan in May 1993. When Mumme left Valdosta State for Kentucky, Holgorsen branched out and coached at Mississippi College and Wingate University before reuniting with Leach at Texas Tech in 2000.

After the 2007 season, Holgorsen left Lubbock to be offensive coordinator at Houston. His unit finished third in the nation in total offense in 2008 before leading the country in the same category in 2009. From there he took the same position at Oklahoma State and created similar results as the Cowboys led the nation in total offense in 2010. Holgorsen's next move took him to Morgantown to become head coach at West Virginia University. The Mountaineers won the Big East in his first season. The following season, West Virginia moved to the Big 12 and proceeded to score forty points a game on their new conference opponents.

The Mountaineers' success during Holgorsen's first two seasons in Morgantown was aided by an offensive line directed by former Iowa Wesleyan teammate Bill Bedenbaugh. The stint at West Virginia was not the first that they spent together on their respective coaching trails. Bedenbaugh's first coaching job was at Valdosta State in 1996 before he was reunited with Holgorsen at Texas Tech from 2000 to 2006. From 2007 to 2010, Bedenbaugh directed the offensive line at University of Arizona. He left West Virginia to coach the offensive line at Oklahoma before the 2013 season.

Mumme's son and former Iowa Wesleyan ballboy, Matt, searching for a vocation after his detasseling career failed to get off the ground, also followed his father into coaching. He is currently the head coach at LaGrange College after making stops at Southeastern Louisiana, New Mexico State, McMurry University, and Davidson College.

Clearly, Iowa Wesleyan's former coaches and players found a passion for offense in Mount Pleasant. However, a number of them also found their calling as strength coaches. Mumme's first strength coach, Dan Wirth, went on to become the Director of Strength and Conditioning for University of Arizona's entire athletic program in 1994, a position he continues to hold. A year into Wirth's tenure, he brought on former Iowa Wesleyan linebacker Marc Hill to serve as strength coach for the Wildcats' basketball team, a group that won the national title in 1997. In 1999, Hill joined Mumme in Lexington to become strength coach for the football team. He is currently executive associate athletic director at University of Kentucky.

Tiger defensive end Doug Elisaia also found passion for strength and conditioning at Iowa Wesleyan. After stints at McPherson College and Wayne State University, he joined Hill at Kentucky in 2002 before moving on to Salt Lake City where he has been University of Utah's director of strength and conditioning for the past eight years.

The success of Mumme's former players at Iowa Wesleyan is hardly limited to athletic endeavors. After graduation, Dustin Dewald returned to Copperas Cove to join the family business: home building. Dewald's father was starting a business that coincided with the housing boom that blossomed around Fort Hood as troops returned from Desert Storm and the fallout from the savings-and-loan crises began to subside. Four years later Dewald started his own business, Dustin Dewald Custom Homes, drawing on his father and grandfather's experiences as well as his own renovating his home in Mount Pleasant.

Marcus Washington, whose admission to Iowa Wesleyan created a veritable battleground between Mumme and admissions, fell in love with school when he came to Mount Pleasant. After graduation he went on to earn his doctorate in school psychology from the University of Iowa and is now a school psychologist in the state of Minnesota.

Pati Pati, a safety out of American Samoa, returned home after graduation to begin a career in education. In 2005 he was named the American Samoa Teacher of the Year. He also served as head football coach, looking to provide his students and players with the same opportunities he had at Iowa Wesleyan.

The list of former Tigers who went on to find professional success outside of football after graduation goes on. Many point to their formative years in Mount Pleasant as the place where they discovered their potential as people and what it took to thrive in their chosen fields. Mumme's tenure as Iowa Welseyan's head football coach created a veritable tree of success that has branched out in a variety of directions. Despite the individual legacies and stories that they continue to write, the trunk to the tree of success that they share and how well they worked together on the field while the ball was in the air is a legacy that has changed football.

Holgorsen put it best as he assessed the variety of schematic approaches found across the football landscape: "There's a high percentage of people that have a little of the Hal Mumme system, whether they know it or don't know it, and that started in a gym in Mount Pleasant. A lot of the things you see in college football today were drawn on a board for the very first time at Iowa Wesleyan College in the early '90s."

INDEX

E
Eagles (Central Methodist University), 42, 46
Edwards, Chris, 30–31, 39, 41–42, 49, 56
Edwards, LaVell, viii, 7, 45, 64–65, 90
Elisaia, Doug, 148
Elon University, xi
Emerson, Ralph Waldo, vii
Ephraim, Utah, 97
Erickson, Dennis, viii, 91–94
Esiason, Boomer, 100
Eureka College, 80
Evans, Bob, 18, 56

F
Falcons (Concordia University), 82–83, 130
Fanoga, Mike, xii, 50, 97–99, 117–118, 140
Feldman, Bruce, xiii
Florida, ix, 52–53, 89, 100
Fort Scott Community College, 59
French, Roger, viii
Fry, Hayden, viii, 15–16, 20, 25
Funderburk, Lance, 146

G
Gallup, New Mexico, xi
Gardner, Lance, 44
Gatewood, Dennis, 18, 68, 73
Georgia, 4, 145, 147
Gratia, Al, 123
Gratia, Ursula, 123
Gratia Hupp, Suzanna, 123
Graves, Lynn, 49
Greenville College, 40–42, 44–45, 62, 79–80, 120
Grey Cup, 89
Griffin III, Robert, 7
Griffith, Michael, 123
Grinnell College, 39–40, 74

H
Hall, Dereck, 31–32, 39, 41, 56, 79, 83
Hamilton, Dean, 15
Hammond, Louisiana, xi
Harding College, 110–112, 115, 125
Harlon Hill Trophy, 106, 146
Hatcher, Chris, 146
Hawkeyes (University of Iowa), viii, 9, 15–16, 25, 42, 105
Heisman Trophy, 65, 106, 146
Henderson, Kalen, xii

157

Welch, Jack, 7
West Alabama, University of, 50, 98
West Texas State University, 6, 7, 15
West Virginia University, 4, 147
Western Athletic Conference (WAC), 7
Wichita Falls, Texas, 110
Wildcats (University of Arizona), 148
Wildcats (University of Kentucky), 146
Wiley, John, 117, 118
William Penn University, 35
Wingate University, 147
Wirth, Dan, 15, 25–28, 148
Wolves (Joliet Junior College), 21
World League of American Football, 89
Wright, John, 21–22, 110, 140

Y
Yung, Bill, 6, 7, 12, 40

CPSIA information can be obtained
at www.ICGtesting.com
Printed in the USA
BVHW03s1433150218
508094BV00003B/300/P